SEEKING WISE COUNSEL

Seeking Wise Counsel

How to Find Help for Your Problems

DAVID STOOP, PH.D.

SERVANT PUBLICATIONS
ANN ARBOR, MICHIGAN

Vine Books is an imprint of Servant Publications especially designed to serve evangelical Christians.

Servant Publications—Mission Statement
We are dedicated to publishing books that spread the gospel of Jesus Christ, help Christians to live in accordance with that gospel, promote renewal in the church, and bear witness to Christian unity.

Published in association with the literary agency of Alive Communications, Inc., 7680 Goddard Street, Suite 200, Colorado Springs, Colorado 80920.

Published by Servant Publications
P.O. Box 8617
Ann Arbor, Michigan 48107
www.servantpub.com

Cover design: Uttley/DouPonce/Gilbert DesignWorks, Sisters, Oregon

02 03 04 05 10 9 8 7 6 5 4 3 2 1

Printed in the United States of America
ISBN 1-56955-298-3

Library of Congress Cataloging-in-Publication Data

Stoop, David A.
   Seeking wise counsel : how to find help for your problems / David Stoop.
      p. cm.
   Includes bibliographical references.
   ISBN 1-56955-298-3 (alk. paper)
   1. Counseling–Religious aspects–Christianity.   I. Title.
BR115.C69S76 2002
253.5–dc21

2002010581

Acknowledgments

My wife, Jan, is really my coauthor for all my books, and I thank her for her help and encouragement. I also want to thank Michael Lyles, M.D., for his help with the chapter on medications, and Pastor Craig Lockwood, for his help on the chapter on healing prayer.

I especially want to thank Bert Ghezzi and all of his staff at Servant Publications. Bert is not only a fine writer and editor; he is a good friend as well.

Contents

Part I
Nonclinical Helpers

Part II
Clinical Helpers

Part III
Other Paths for Finding Help

ONE

Life Will Be Difficult–at Times!

At some point in our lives, every one of us will need wise counsel from someone else. There will be times when we must reach outside ourselves to find someone who can hear and help us understand our pain. We may be facing a tragic loss through death, divorce, or illness; we may need help resolving marital, parenting, or other relational problems; or we may be struggling with important spiritual issues. The truth is, because we are human we will need help moving through and getting beyond painful stages in our lives. Encouragement and words of wisdom from a godly source will strengthen and guide us at these times.

Personally, I have not always sought help when I should have. There have been times when I faced deep crises and tried to handle them on my own. But there were other times when I learned important lessons about the miraculous power of God as he worked through another person in my life—one who helped me face and deal with my struggle by sharing godly wisdom with me. So I can tell you from personal experience—don't go it alone! And especially don't go it alone just because you think the problem is trivial. Don't forgo help because you feel you shouldn't need help or because you don't want to bother someone else with what seem like minor concerns.

I have never forgotten the one bit of wise counsel that I received before getting married. I went to the dean of men at the Christian college I was attending. I thought that he would have some wisdom and key insights based on his years of experience in the realm of relationships. After all, he was in the business of dealing with young college age men who were probably thinking about getting married as much as or even more than, they were thinking about their academic training. I envisioned meeting with this man and learning all that I needed to know to be the husband I wanted to be for Jan.

I told the dean that Jan and I were getting married that summer. Before I could ask him about everything on my mind, he said, "Well, I have one thing to say, if you are asking about how a marriage works." I was taken aback by his quick response but was all ears as I awaited his wisdom. Here is what he said: "Dave, I've found that a good husband never forgets to open the door for his wife." After a moment's pause, I said, "That's it?" and he said, "That's it. That's the only advice I have to give."

I wouldn't advise a couple contemplating marriage to base their relationship on those simple words, but the truth is that for over forty-five years I have been opening the door for Jan. I have never forgotten the dean's advice. It was truly wise counsel for me!

Sometimes we can turn to our parents for wise counsel. Sadly, though, I didn't get counsel of any kind from my own dad or mom, wise or otherwise. My dad was always too busy or too tired and my mom was in her own world. I learned to never bother them with my problems. I kept my struggles and feelings to myself and toughed it out on my own. Not very good preparation for life, since inevitably life comes saturated with difficulties.

I had to learn how and when to seek the counsel of others and this turned out to be a difficult journey for me. Eventually I learned how to find counsel that is wise and right for me, since not all counsel is wise, and not all help is right for everyone. Over the years, I've discovered that most of us need guidance to discern how to seek the kind of counsel that is best for our individual situations.

Finding help for our problems today is quite different than it was thirty or forty years ago. I remember the problems Jan and I had early in our marriage. Yes, we still had problems even though I was consistently opening the door for her! We sometimes refer to the early years of our married life as our great tribulation. We felt we had no one to whom we could turn. It was not fashionable to go to counselors then, nor were there many counselors available. Very few of those were known as Christian counselors. We didn't even think of going to our pastor because I was one of the pastors on the church staff. Letting on you had a problem was not acceptable. Our parents were not around and our friends had never shared their difficulties with us so we didn't feel free to share with them. We thought we had to tough it out and thankfully we survived. Opening the door definitely helped!

But it would have been a lot less painful if we'd had some wise help. We knew of few books on the subject of marriage, and not many of those were written from the Christian perspective.

When a crisis comes or problems hit, where should we go for help? Do we go to a professional counselor? Or can we find help in a book or video series? What about talking to a close friend or to a pastor? Whom can we trust and how do we know what is best? How do we counteract the tendency to muddle through on our own, feeling that keeping it all inside is the best and least threatening thing to do?

Many people do as I did in those early years, dealing with their difficulties on their own. Or they guiltily listen to those who have told them to just trust God. They begin to wonder, "Why can't I have the faith to get through this? After all, isn't God sufficient for my every need? Do I really need input from someone else?" These are valid questions and Christians often ask them when faced with a problem. Let's look at what the Bible says about this issue.

The Holy Spirit—the Divine Counselor

Some passages in the Bible seem to suggest that God alone will take care of our problems. One of these passages is found in 1 Thessalonians 5:23-24. Paul writes, "Now may the God of peace make you holy in every way, and may your whole spirit and soul and body be kept blameless until that day when our Lord Jesus Christ comes again. God, who calls you, is faithful; he will do this." God is the one who will make you holy, and he will keep every part of you blameless. He will do it! But most of us don't experience this and begin to feel guilty because we don't trust him more. Let's take a closer look at God's plan for us. (Philippians 1:6 and Hebrews 10:14 are also relevant to this discussion.)

A situation from my years as a young associate pastor taught me a lot about how God helps us with our problems. A woman in the congregation was married to an alcoholic. She attended church faithfully and her husband came once in awhile. There were a great number of people praying for this man to commit his life to Jesus and give up his drinking. Many of us believed that if you had a problem, you just needed to have more faith and God would deliver you from it. If you were not delivered, it was because your faith was weak.

One Sunday night, at the end of the service, the senior pastor gave an altar call. He invited anyone to come forward who wanted help with problems or who wanted to give their life to the Lord Jesus. You could almost hear a collective gasp as this man stepped into the aisle and walked to the front of the church. As we prayed with him, there were many who cried tears of joy at what God was going to do in his life.

The senior pastor asked me to follow up on this man, and for several weeks he did wonderfully well. He was kinder to his wife and children and he quit drinking. But about three weeks later, we got a panicky call from his wife saying he was drinking again. I went out to the home and talked and prayed with him. He was remorseful and made all kinds of promises. I told him I would come back the next day and we would talk more when he was sober. I did, and he was genuinely repentant. We prayed and left it up to God to take care of him.

Then his wife called again, and a third time, and we didn't know what to do. We just prayed more and didn't understand why God wasn't taking care of the situation. Soon after, the family stopped coming to our church. Perhaps they were embarrassed, thinking people would judge their faith as weak. I saw the wife about a year later and learned her husband was doing great. The difference, she said, was that he had started going to Alcoholics Anonymous meetings and there found the help he needed to face and overcome his problem.

I learned from that experience that there is much more in 1 Thessalonians that might help me better understand how God accomplishes his work in us. For example, at the beginning of the book, Paul says, "For when we brought you the Good News, it was not only with words but also with power, for the Holy Spirit gave you full assurance that what we said was true. And you know that the way we lived among you was further proof of the truth of our message" (1:5). For the Thessalonians to become believers, two things had to happen: Paul had to speak the Good News to them, and the Holy Spirit had to work in their hearts and minds. God chose to use Paul in a collaborative effort with the Holy Spirit.

The same is usually true for us when we need help. A collaborative effort will take place between a people-helper (a counselor, friend, or pastor, for example) and the Holy Spirit. This is what the alcoholic husband eventually experienced.

The First Letter to the Thessalonians reveals at least five points that are features of this collaborative effort between the Holy Spirit and Paul, as God worked in the lives of the Thessalonians. These same five points can also be part of what we experience when we get help for our problems. Let's see what the Thessalonians faced.

1. *Confronting problems may be extremely painful.*
Paul reminds the Thessalonians twice that they had experienced pain and suffering as they moved toward their goal of following Christ. He says: "You received the message with joy from the Holy Spirit in spite of the severe suffering it brought you" (1:6). And then he says to those who believed: "Dear

brothers and sisters, you suffered persecution from your own countrymen" (2:14). Suffering and persecution accompanied the action of God in their lives. Even people close to the Thessalonians misunderstood, people they expected would surely comprehend.

When we start to work through a crisis or begin to face our problem, there will be suffering on our part. This pain will be compounded by those we thought would understand but don't. Growth involves pain. Change involves suffering. Moving forward may lead to misunderstanding. But in seeking help we stay the course and hold on as we experience the collaborative effort between the Holy Spirit and those we have turned to for help.

2. Facing problems requires support from others.
God created us to operate in relationship with him and with each other. We are not made for isolation. Therefore, his plan to help us will usually play out within the context of a relationship with another person. Why was it so important for Paul to send Timothy to Thessalonica to strengthen the Thessalonians? Paul writes, "Finally, when we could stand it no longer, we decided that I should stay alone in Athens, and we sent Timothy to visit you.... We sent him to strengthen you, to encourage you in your faith, and to keep you from becoming disturbed by the troubles you were going through" (3:1-3). Paul knew they needed to work together; he sent Timothy to encourage and help in that process.

Obviously, Paul didn't expect God to make everything work out for the Thessalonians without human help. He adds this admonition to them as he comes to the end of the letter: "So encourage each other and build each other up, just as you are already doing" (5:11). Paul sent Timothy because he thought that they might not be helping each other enough. When Timothy gave Paul a good report, Paul knew it was because they were taking care of each other. God, the Holy Spirit, was at work in and through each of them as they did the work of helping.

3. *Facing problems involves being teachable.*

Sometimes we don't know how to resolve a problem or deal with hurts because we don't know what to look for. We need someone to help us uncover all the components of our situation, to learn what we need to know, to see what we need to see. In short, we need someone to teach us and lead us. Paul did this with the Thessalonians. He writes, "Finally, dear brothers and sisters, we urge you in the name of the Lord Jesus to live in a way that pleases God, as we have taught you" (4:1).

Paul not only refers to what he has taught them, he refers also to how he lived while with them. His life had been an object lesson designed to demonstrate to the Thessalonians how they were to live together. Paul was a teacher, and he was a mentor to them as well. That was Paul's part in the collaborative effort with the Holy Spirit for the sake of the Thessalonians. He even says, "You imitated both us and the Lord" (1:6).

4. *Facing problems may involve some form of reparenting.*

The prophet Isaiah sets out an important principle for us as we seek help. He says, "Listen to me, all who hope for deliverance—all who seek the Lord! Consider the quarry from which you were mined, the rock from which you were cut!" (Isaiah 51:1). When we seek the Lord's deliverance from a life-problem or for healing from past hurts, Isaiah suggests that we begin by looking at our roots.

When I was a boy, my dad's friends would often say about me, "Oh, he's a chip off the old block." They meant I not only looked like my dad, but I acted like him as well. They could tell I was his son. If we want to better understand ourselves—and we need to understand who we are in order to successfully face our problems—Isaiah says that we should look to the block from which we were chipped, the rock from which we were cut. To make certain we understand his meaning, Isaiah then says, "Yes, think about your ancestors...." (verse 2).

Why does Isaiah say this? I think he knows that no one comes from a perfect family, or is ever parented perfectly. If we were, research suggests that perfect parenting would create its own set of problems. Many of the problems we struggle with as adults are the result of destructive patterns that were set in motion when we were children. So every one of us can benefit from looking at our past and then allowing someone to love us as God loves us. On a certain level, this person might even become something of a mother or father to us, helping to repair some of the damage from our past. This is what Paul did with the Thessalonians.

Note Paul's approach as he worked among the Thessalonians: "We were as gentle among you as a mother feeding and caring for her own children. We loved you so much that we gave you not only God's Good News but our own lives, too" (1 Thessalonians 2:7-8). He is saying that for the Thessalonians to become what God wanted them to be, he had to "mother" them.

Paul continues: "And you know that we treated each of you as a father treats his own children. We pleaded with you, encouraged you, and urged you to live your lives in a way that God would consider worthy" (2:11-12). He both mothered and fathered them. He was, in a sense, reparenting them so that they could personally realize God's love.

Wise counsel will often come from someone who cares for us and in some healthy way acts toward us in a motherly or fatherly manner. Paul says he mothered by loving, caring, and feeding the Thessalonians—never asking for anything from them. He fathered them by encouraging, pleading, and urging them to do what they were to do. He was filling in the gaps, providing the love and direction they needed.

5. *Facing problems always requires change in me.*

Finally, Paul gets very specific as he instructs the Thessalonians in how to live. He gives them a long list of the things they were to do and the things they were to avoid. For example, they were not to judge another brother or sister's behavior—they were to look only at themselves. Sometimes when we face a problem, someone can come along and give specific advice that resolves the situation. Similarly, in 1 Thessalonians 5:12, Paul gives guidelines tailored to meet the needs of the Thessalonians.

If this whole process of finding help—or for the Thessalonians, growing in faith—were all up to God, then why all these directives? Obviously, the answer is that God chooses to work through others. We seek help from others knowing that God is at work through his Holy Spirit in the process.

When we finish the list Paul gives, we come to the verses we started with (1 Thessalonians 5:22, 24). But now we have them in context and can see that they represent a promise. It's as if Paul is saying, "Do all these things, remember what we taught you, don't be afraid of pain and suffering, and lean on each other, knowing that God is at work in your midst. God is faithful; he will work in you through this process!"

But to whom do I go when seeking help? Who's going to be my Paul or Timothy? Turning to just anyone isn't the solution, nor does it seem safe emotionally. If I'm going to get wise counsel, and if I am going to share something about my problems and myself with someone else, I need to choose that person very carefully.

Today we are blessed to have all kinds of professional Christian counselors: lay and peer counselors in our church who have been trained to be helpers; pastors with counseling skills; pastors who can direct us; and, of course, Christian psychologists, therapists, and psychiatrists. In addition, there are now so many self-help books, tapes, and videos that it may be confusing as to which offers the best advice. So where do we turn when we need wise counsel?

Two

Seeking Wise Counsel

Once you realize that you can't face your problem alone, you might feel frustrated as you try to decide where to turn. You could find yourself with too many options and no idea how to discern what is best for your situation. That's a valid concern.

My task in this book is to help you sort through all the counseling options and other resources available today. I'll give you guidelines and information on the various kinds of assistance you might encounter. And I'll help you decide the level of intervention you need based on the type of problem you face.

To assist you in that task, I want to introduce you to people involved in four different situations. These four situations are compilations, typical of the problems I see every day in my counseling office. The first case involves a parenting issue. The second concerns a couple whose marriage is about to be destroyed because of an addiction. The third involves a single woman who is having a crisis at work that has triggered a crisis in her faith. And the fourth involves a distressed marriage where one partner is not functioning very well.

There are other crises we could have used—loss of a child, boundary issues, financial disasters—but I have chosen these four and will use each of these case studies throughout the book to clarify how various types of counsel can help in different situations. We'll also consider how some resources will not help in certain situations. Let's meet our people.

A Crisis in the Parent-Child Relationship

Ty and Ellie are the parents of two beautiful daughters. Brittany is fifteen and Ashley is twelve. Both girls have been a delight for Ty and Ellie to raise—that is, up until recently. The girls have been very active in church, participating in youth groups and taking on leadership roles as well. Ashley has played guitar for several years and is now participating with the worship team in the junior high program. She loves being in front of the group and admits she likes being noticed, especially by some of the boys. But she also says that she does it to please the Lord.

The family has attended this church for only nine months, having just moved to the community. Ty had a promotion that required relocation, and the change brought them not only to a new church, but also to new schools. Ty and Ellie were concerned about how Brittany would adjust to the move. She was just starting high school and in this town, all the kids went to one huge central high school. Brittany didn't know anyone there and she had never attended such a large school before. But she seemed to fit in right away and Mom and Dad were pleased that her new friends were from the church the family attended.

Ashley was starting junior high, and her new school wasn't too large. Both Ty and Ellie felt she would adjust more easily. But the adjustment had been difficult for Ashley, at least until she started taking part in the worship team at church.

Ty was overwhelmed by his new position and the hours he

put in were much longer than at his previous job. As a result, he often missed dinner, and when he finally did come home, he was exhausted and irritable. He was happy with the promotion, but felt he really had to prove himself in the new position. Frequently, his family took second best in terms of his time.

Ellie, who had always depended on Ty for help with the girls, now found herself coping alone with much of the parenting responsibilities. She was frustrated with Ashley, who was becoming more moody and rebellious. Ellie felt that Ashley's behavior was related primarily to the beginning of puberty, and so she didn't tell Ty much about her frustration with their second daughter. She also didn't want to add to Ty's stress.

But the problem came to a head when Ashley brought home her midterm report card. Ty and Ellie were shocked to find that Ashley, previously an A student, was failing in two subjects. On top of that, Ashley had been lying about her grades and her homework, stating that she was doing her homework when in reality she wasn't. Her report card also noted that her failing grades were related not only to her failure to turn in homework, but also to some poor test scores.

Ty and Ellie were confused. They had never faced anything like this with either daughter. They remembered, too, that when they were kids, they would have done their homework, and certainly wouldn't have lied to their parents about it. Up to this point, parenting had been rather easy and very satisfying. Now they were faced with something they didn't know how to handle.

What were they to do? Should they find a counselor for Ashley? What had other parents done in situations like this? They needed help! But where should they start?

A Marital Crisis and Addiction

Sarah is a forty-three-year-old woman who has been married for eighteen years to Gary. They are childless by choice, a decision they made before they married. Both had worked hard at developing their careers and they liked traveling together. Each year they vacationed in a different part of the world and enjoyed experiencing a variety of cultures. Their travels have provided shared times that have been very satisfying.

For the past year, Sarah has been under a lot of pressure at her job. Her company has been in a financial crunch, and Sarah is the head of the accounting department. As the company has stretched its dollars to meet expenses, Sarah has had to put in extra hours.

At the same time, things have been going well with Gary's job. Business has been booming, and Gary's position as vice-president of sales and marketing has been nearly on autopilot. Everything Gary has tried has worked, and many of his ideas have succeeded far beyond projections. He's been traveling a lot, meeting with his sales reps, and basically just keeping his team focused on expansion.

Recently, Gary has seemed preoccupied whenever he is at home. Since Sarah had been working more hours, he was free to come and go, and seemed to go more often than usual. One evening, Sarah came home earlier than expected and Gary wasn't home. When he did return, he acted defensive about where he had been. Sarah began to wonder what was going on.

A couple of weeks later, strange phone calls started coming to the house, further raising Sarah's concerns. She looked through Gary's things, including his briefcase, and found local credit charges at a massage parlor and a couple of porno-graphic CDs. She was shocked and heartbroken at the same time. She checked his e-mails and "history" on his computer and found that he had spent a lot of time at pornographic sites and had even e-mailed women from some of the sites. She confronted Gary. He not only confessed to the use of pornography and massage parlors but also told her that he was having an affair with someone he met in an Internet chat room.

Sarah, enraged, ordered him out of the house. She felt she had lost the man she had married, and that he had become a stranger to her. She also called an attorney and made an appointment to start divorce proceedings. What else was she supposed to do? He had betrayed her!

Had Sarah done the right thing in asking him to leave? Should they have tried marital counseling? Maybe Gary should find a counselor? But what type? Did Gary turn to pornography and another woman because she'd been too busy to notice? Did she need medication to get through the intense stress she was experiencing? These, and other questions, flooded her mind. Obviously, she needed help! But what kind of help would be most useful?

A Crisis With Work and a Crisis of Faith
Anne is a twenty-seven-year old single woman for whom life has been pretty good. She was raised in a Christian home and had a comfortable relationship with both her mom and dad. She was dating a wonderful young man from her church and they were beginning to talk tentatively about marriage.

Anne's college experience had been wonderful. She

attended a solid Christian school and majored in business. She had made great friends, many of whom she still saw. Her professors recognized her potential and helped her make career choices, even using their connections to set her up in a job with a great company.

When Anne started working, things continued to fall into place. Promotions came at the right time. Raises were more than she expected. She was considered one of the prime young managers in the company. Her bosses liked her and believed in her, and she felt very secure on her career track.

Anne was involved in her church. She was a teacher in the junior high department and served as a deaconess as well. People enjoyed her and several of the older couples sometimes invited her over for meals and showed an interest in her romantic relationships.

But things changed suddenly when the company brought in a new manager to head up Anne's division. Almost instantly, there was friction between Anne and her new manager. The friction had now grown to the point where Anne started to fear for her job. When she talked with her old boss, it was clear that her current boss was the "fair-haired boy" of the management team, and that her fears were not unfounded. They were grooming the new man for bigger and better things. She was told to make peace with him or else. She was on thin ice because word of her conflict had already reached upper management.

Anne was scared. Nothing like this had ever happened to her before. She didn't know what to do. Her fears started to affect her relationship with her boyfriend. They began to fight a lot. When she tried to talk to her dad, he just gave her some platitudes that weren't helpful. What scared Anne even more was that her faith seemed powerless in the face of what was happening. She felt very alone, as if God had deserted her. Was God only real for her when circumstances were good?

Many of the things she had previously believed about her relationship with God weren't working now. It seemed that no matter how much she prayed, nothing changed. She tried to read her Bible regularly, but found it dry and empty. She realized she was angry with God for not protecting her in this situation. She felt like she'd been set up. And when her new boss warned her that she was about to lose her job, she was in a panic. She didn't know where God was, and she certainly didn't know how to get back on track with him.

Where should she focus? Did Anne need help coping with the new boss? Should she look for a new job now? Or did she need to talk to someone about her faith and get these questions settled? She knew she needed help, but where should she begin?

A Marriage in Crisis

Scott and Marianne have been married for seven years. They are both thirty-six years old and had been very independent before they married. They have a three-year-old son they thoroughly enjoy. They have both been active in their church and faithful in attendance. The pastor and his wife have been good friends ever since he presided at their wedding. But things have been changing lately and not for the better.

Marianne has been doing great with her job. She had an excellent review and a good raise recently and enjoys her work. She wishes she could be home more with their son, but

Scott and Marianne agreed when they married that they both needed to work.

On the other hand, Scott hasn't been doing well. He had lost two jobs, and each time it had taken him several months to find a new one. Marianne remembered that before they were married, he had changed jobs a lot, but Scott had a good explanation each time. She didn't know then that Scott made several of those job changes because he'd been fired. She was beginning to see a very disturbing pattern, especially because of some of the behaviors that accompanied Scott's job problems.

"If he'd help more at home, I think I could adjust," Marianne said. Scott was a genuine couch potato. He watched TV nonstop from the time he got home from work until he went to bed. He still went to church with her, but all he seemed to care about was the church's baseball team. He had to attend in order to play on the team. When Marianne asked him to help with the dishes, or with their son, he griped and complained so much about being tired that she eventually quit asking him to do much.

She had also picked up on a pattern related to his work. Six months into a job, Scott would begin to complain about his boss. He said he felt unappreciated at work—that no one gave him any credit for what he did. Eventually he would have a problem with a coworker. This was usually one who was performing well, and who would get the promotion that Scott wanted. Usually, the second time someone else got a promotion he wanted, he would pick a fight with his boss over it. Scott always ended up quitting or getting fired.

When he was unemployed, he insisted that their son go to day care. Scott claimed he needed to concentrate on looking for a new job but Marianne thought most of those days were nonproductive. He didn't land a job, and the chores around the house were all left for her to take care of when she got home from work.

Sure enough, what Marianne feared happened. Scott was fired again and the cycle began anew. Marianne didn't think she could handle it one more time. "After all," she thought, "I'm just like a single mom as it is—what would be worse if I left Scott?" But that wasn't really an option. She valued the vows she had made when they married and she didn't intend to file for divorce, even though the thought of not having to deal with Scott felt very freeing.

If Marianne couldn't stand staying, and wouldn't consider leaving, what was she to do? Scott refused to see a counselor and they'd already talked to the pastor. Was Scott depressed? Was this a pattern he learned from childhood? Would he ever change? She needed help even if Scott wasn't willing to talk to anyone!

Finding Help

Where does each of these people find help? How will they find wise counsel? Does any of them need a professional, and if so, why? If you have questions like these, then you've come to the right place. This book will help you find the guidance you need, and also tell you the pros and cons of each choice available to you. We will continue to look at these four case studies, and use them to determine the best way to find counsel.

In chapters 3 through 5 we'll look at the nonclinical resources available. In chapters 6 through 9 we'll look at the professional options, including the use of medication. Finally, in chapters 10 and 11, we'll look at special ways to apply the spiritual discipline of prayer which, though necessary anytime, is especially important during life's difficulties.

Part I

Nonclinical Helpers

THREE

Finding Help in Books, Tapes, and Videos

When trouble hits, we often turn first to a book. We head to the bookstore and search the shelves to see if someone has written about the issue we are struggling with.

Frequently, we find numerous self-help books addressing our concern. If we need help with our kids, there are stacks of books on the market. If we need help with our marriages, the selection is going to be difficult because there are so many choices. If we have questions about our faith, all kinds of resources are at our fingertips. Our problem won't be finding help; it will be in discerning which resources will actually be helpful.

The question always comes up: Do we limit ourselves to books written by Christians? Or can we find a secular book that will prove to be helpful as well? Should we look in both Christian and secular bookstores? How do we decide which books, whether Christian or secular, are the best? Not everyone who writes a book is going to have the same values we have, including some Christian writers. All too often we assume that if a publisher went to the trouble and expense of publishing the book, the author must know something about the topic. Usually authors do, but sometimes they can be off base.

I know of a best-seller in the Christian market that was written by authors who have become well-known "authorities" on their subject. But their advice has been very controversial, has divided church congregations, and has caused harm in some families. At the same time, their insights have helped other families and they have a faithful group of supporters. How do I know if their advice would be appropriate in my situation, especially if I felt hopeless about what I was facing? Obviously, we need discernment when we turn to the impersonal world of books, tapes, and videos.

Sometimes, our Bible study group will pick a book or video series to discuss. These can be seen as preventive measures, answering some of our questions before a problem arises. I know people who have watched a video series in their small group and then some time later faced the problem addressed in the videos. They went back and watched the series again to find the help they needed.

Many videotape sets are available, both in bookstores and on the Internet, and often a church library has copies we can borrow. A video seems more personal because we can actually see the expert we are turning to for help. Videos can also be more helpful than a book because they encourage interaction with the other people watching the video with us. More than one person can watch a video, while only one person at a time can read a given book.

One of the shortcomings of turning to a book is that too often we don't discuss what we've read with anyone else. When this occurs, we're limited in our application of what we've discovered. When it comes to implementing our newfound insight, we may be unable to put anything into action. We may be just as paralyzed after reading the book as before, only now we have additional knowledge and feel guilty because we cannot act upon it. Audiotapes present the same problem. It's too easy to listen to them in the privacy of our car or home, and not talk with someone about what we're learning.

While we are grateful for the various resources out there, our problem boils down to picking and choosing which ones to use (a problem that often seems more solvable than the life problem we face). So how does one decide where to turn? Will books, tapes, or videos be the right answer in every circumstance? Let's see how the people in our four scenarios handled these questions.

Help for Parents: Ty and Ellie's Experience

How did Ty and Ellie make their choices? First they went to Internet sites that sold books and looked at reader comments on those about raising teenagers. They made notes on several books that received good reviews. Next, list in hand, they headed to both Christian and secular bookstores. In each place they found several books on raising teenagers, even a book on how to help your kids with grades. Needless to say, they grabbed that one.

They checked the back cover of each book to see if anyone they knew of and respected had endorsed it. They also looked through the table of contents, read the introduction, checked to see if the book had a topical index, and then read bits here and there to see if it was written in a way they could understand. This sort of evaluation will tell you if a book is related to the issue you're dealing with, and if it is written in an accessible style.

Ty and Ellie bought four of the best and went home feeling as if they were doing something to address their problem with their daughter.

Once home, they divided up the books and set up a reading schedule. When they found something interesting or relevant to their problem, they marked it in the book and made some notes on the side of the page. After a couple of weeks, they had read all of the books and learned important things about kids and lying, the needs of teenagers, how families work, and how they needed to put Ashley's problem into the larger context of what had changed in their family this past year.

Ty and Ellie took their reading one step further, and this made quite a difference in their ability to find wise counsel. They not only read the books and marked them up with their comments and questions, they also made it a point to talk about what they had learned from their reading. They asked each other questions such as what elements of the move had caused the sort of stress that negatively affected Ashley.

This talking together about their reading helped to put them "on the same page" as they changed the ways they worked with both girls. In addition, it greatly enhanced their general knowledge of what was involved in raising teenagers. They had a better understanding of what their girls were going through and how the girls' experience differed from their own at that age.

Help When We Don't Understand: Sarah's Experience

What about Sarah? Her husband, Gary, was gone and she was struggling not only with the knowledge of his affair but also of his secret life of pornography. Can she benefit from a book, a video, or an audiotape? Sarah was broken emotionally from what she had discovered about Gary and she was also humiliated, particularly by his involvement with pornography. She didn't talk with anyone about that aspect of his problem. But she found a video series on pornography at a Christian bookstore and purchased it. She said something to the clerk about buying it for the church library and then hurried home to watch the series by herself.

By the time she finished the videos, she was overwhelmed by the magnitude of Gary's problems. In some ways she felt better knowing what she was dealing with, but in other ways she felt more hopeless than ever. Her knowledge of the problem had grown immensely but, at the same time, she felt more alone than she had before watching the series.

That wasn't all bad. What Sarah was encountering was the limitation of a book, video, or tape. Unless we discuss with others the insights we've gained from these resources, our ability to act may stay the same or even feel diminished in some way. At this stage, Sarah needed people to walk alongside her, perhaps more than she needed information. The most painful thing she could experience at this point was her aloneness, not her lack of knowledge.

No Help Here: Anne's Experience

One day, Anne was having lunch with an old friend. She decided she would broach the subject of her personal struggle by pretending the situation involved a coworker at the office. She laid out the circumstances without too much detail, lest her friend suspect she was talking about herself. As she finished, her companion zeroed in on the hypothetical coworker's struggle with faith. She recommended a helpful tape series she had just heard. Anne made a note of the series and where she could buy it, and then, relieved, changed the subject.

Anne followed up on the recommendation and listened carefully to each tape. As she listened in her car and at home, Anne found the speaker made some points that were helpful, but she questioned a number of other points. She found herself arguing with the tapes. Even though each tape answered some of her questions, Anne always ended up with more new, unanswered questions. She needed to talk with someone, but since she was still embarrassed by her situation, she decided to just listen to the tapes again.

The Limits and Benefits of Books, Tapes, and Videos

It is important to remember that there is a real limit to the help available from these impersonal forms of assistance. As we'll see more clearly in the next chapter, God made us for relationship, not only with him, but with each other. Since books, tapes, and videos are impersonal, we need to understand their limitations.

But what are their benefits? Ty and Ellie needed additional information regarding how to raise teenagers, and how family changes and stress affect individual members of the family, especially the children. In large part, they had an informational deficit and the books they read helped to fill that deficit.

In addition, Ty and Ellie did something with the books that brought in the relational aspect of problem-solving—they talked together about their reading. That made their subjective experience more objective. Sometimes they had to reread a section of a book because of the different insights they each received from the same information. As they reread and discussed further, they arrived at a common, more objective understanding of what the author meant and how it could be applied in their situation.

The reading they did also made them feel more confident as parents. Since they discussed what they were reading, they were more in sync with each other as they parented their girls. At this stage of dealing with their problems, reading gave them wise counsel.

But Sarah and Anne had different needs. They had informational deficits but, more urgently, they each needed direct help from others. Both Anne and Sarah felt very alone as they faced their individual problems. They lacked objectivity and were overwhelmed by the subjective experience of their hurt, confusion, and pain. A tape, video, or book might have been helpful at some point, but what they needed first and foremost were other people.

Sarah needed friends to surround her and to pray for her, people she could call at any hour, day or night—whenever she felt she was going to be swallowed up in despair. Anne needed a wise, godly friend she could bounce her questions off and who would raise questions in turn to make Anne think more clearly. Once they had that circle of human support, then books, videos, and tapes would be appropriate, and would fill in some of their gaps of knowledge.

How to Use Books, Tapes, and Videos More Effectively
The following guidelines will help you get the most out of books, tapes, and videos.

First, as you read or watch a video or listen to a tape, focus on the obstacles you face in resolving the problem; don't focus on the problem itself. For example, Ty and Ellie had to change how they viewed their problems with Ashley. Instead of wondering what was wrong with Ashley and how they were going to fix her, they needed to ask questions like, "What were some of the obstacles Ashley faced in telling us about her problem with her grades? Was she afraid of our reaction? Did she feel like she couldn't get our attention? Was she afraid to add to the family stress levels?" As Ty and Ellie asked these types of questions, the books they were reading became more helpful.

In the same way, Anne needed to ask herself, "What are some of the obstacles I'm facing with my new boss? What keeps me from having a better attitude towards him?" These questions shift her away from focusing on the problem to focusing on possible solutions.

Second, boil the problem down to clear specifics. Ty and Ellie had to give up thoughts like, "Our daughter's going to fail!" "Why did we ever move?" or, "Do we need to change schools and get her into a new setting quickly?" Instead, they needed to look at small pieces of the problem. Perhaps they found that their availability to Ashley had become very limited. They had assumed that since she was in a good school and was involved with the church youth group, everything was OK. But now they realized that they should be more available to Ashley, so they looked at some specific things they could do. Ty set up regular time each week to spend alone with her. Ellie decided she needed to be home when Ashley came home; she needed to be available to talk. And she needed to avoid getting sidetracked by Ashley's moods.

Anne had to let go of the idea that the situation with her boss was hopeless. Instead, she needed to define specific steps she could take to improve her work environment. For example, she wondered how she could get to know her new boss better. Instead of staying out of the boss' way, she made a lunch appointment with him and had a couple work-related items to discuss. She also made it a point to ask her boss questions about his background and previous work situations. One piece of information he shared gave Anne new insight into what he was looking for from her, and gave Anne a spark of hope that things could be different.

Third, when dealing with difficult issues, be satisfied with small changes; don't try to resolve the whole situation at once. Rather than try to hit every aspect of their problem, Ty and Ellie decided they would just spend more time with Ashley. Part of that time would focus on her doing her homework.

Anne decided not to push to resolve her faith questions, but to continue to pray and seek God's help. For now, she simply accepted the fact that God was there helping her. She then put her energy into getting to know her new boss, and letting her new boss get to know her better. Once her job situation felt more secure, then she would look more deeply at the questions she had about her relationship with the Lord.

Fourth, and finally, don't get discouraged. If something doesn't work right away, try something different. If the greater availability of Ty and Ellie didn't bring about any change in Ashley's grades and behaviors, then they would look for other obstacles that might be there. If meeting more often with her boss didn't begin to change things, then Anne would look at other possible obstacles. The point is, don't give up. However, when everything you try doesn't seem to work, seek help from someone else. Sometimes we need the eyes of another in order to see what we can't see. We should never be too embarrassed to seek wise counsel from others.

Summary
The value of books, tapes, and **videos** can best be utilized when

- we need added knowledge or information related to our particular problem.
- we have someone with whom we can discuss this information.

FOUR

Wise Counsel From a Friend

We should never underestimate the complexity of life. Certainly Sarah and Marianne would not underestimate the complexity of their marriage problems. They needed more than the impersonal help of a book, tape, or video. And perhaps Ty and Ellie would find they needed more help as well. Because life is complex, we need each other.

I recommend an interesting word study in the Bible: Look up all the passages with the words "one another" in them. When your computer does that, you will find over a hundred verses. Some of these verses are descriptive of something happening and others are about negative behavior that is taking place among "one another." But I count forty-six different passages that list ways we can be supportive of each other. Some are repetitive, but here are the things we are to do with one another:

1. We are to "judge fairly and honestly, and show mercy and kindness to one another" (Zechariah 7:9).
2. We are to be faithful to one another. Malachi says, "Are we not all created by the same God? Then why are we faithless to each other?" (2:10).
3. We are to love one another (John 13:34-35; 15:12, 17; Romans 12:10, 13:8; 1 Thessalonians 4:9; 1 Peter 1:22; 1 John 3:11, 23; 4:7, 11-12; 2 John 1:5).

4. We are to live in harmony with one another (Romans 12:16; 1 Corinthians 1:10; 1 Peter 3:8).

5. Stop passing judgment on one another (Romans 14:13).

6. We are to encourage one another (1 Thessalonians 4:18, 5:11; Hebrews 3:13, 10:25).

7. We are to accept one another (Romans 15:7).

8. We are to greet each other in Christian love (Romans 16:16; 1 Corinthians 16:20; 2 Corinthians 13:12; 1 Peter 5:14).

9. We are to have fellowship with one another (1 John 1:7).

10. We are to serve one another in love, and bear with one another in love (Galatians 5:13; Ephesians 4:2).

11. We are not to provoke or envy one another (1 Corinthians 3:3; Galatians 5:26).

12. We are to forgive one another (Ephesians 4:32; Colossians 3:13).

13. We are to submit to one another (Ephesians 5:21; 1 Peter 5:5).

14. We are to speak, teach, and admonish one another (Ephesians 4:25; Colossians 3:16).

15. We are to spur one another on to greater acts of love (Hebrews 10:24).

16. We are to confess to one another (James 5:16).

17. We are to offer hospitality to one another (1 Peter 4:9).

18. We are to honor one another (Romans 12:10).

19. We are to meet with one another, and speak to one another in psalms, hymns, and spiritual songs (Ephesians 5:19; Hebrews 10:25).

God has made us for himself, but he also made us for "one another." He did that because he knew our lives would be complex. We are not meant to live our lives in isolation. We really do need each other. As you read through the list, you can see all kinds of interaction between people. God's plan is for us to be connected to others. That way, when we are faced with problems, we don't have to face them alone. But the question remains—can we really help one another? The answer seems to be "yes," but we need to be careful.

Seeking a Wise, Trusted Friend

Most counseling is done informally, friend to friend. Research has shown that this can be very effective, especially if that friend has had some training in counseling skills. But there are also those who just know how to provide good counsel; who know how to listen and how to help. People seem to seek them out, for their kind words are like honey—sweet to the soul and healthy for the body (Proverbs 16:24). We will call these people wise friends. Their "words can be life-giving water; [for] words of true wisdom are as refreshing as a bubbling brook" (Proverbs 18:4).

Someone Who Is Godly

The Book of Proverbs gives us good guidelines regarding the kind of person we should turn to when in need of help. First, the person should be godly. Solomon tells us, "The godly person gives wise advice [and] speak[s] words that are helpful" (Proverbs 10:31-32; see 12:26). We may get some good common sense advice from the non-believing friend at the office, but wise, helpful advice often goes beyond common sense. We want to talk to someone who has a heart for God as well as a heart for us.

Someone Who Will Listen

Second, we want to turn to someone who will listen, and not jump in with advice. Solomon says of the hasty, "What a shame, what folly, to give advice before listening to the facts!" (Proverbs 18:13). Often, when we turn to someone for help, they listen to part of what we are saying and then jump in with a plan to solve our problem. In almost every case, we have already considered the advice offered so readily and found it ineffective.

Someone Who Can Understand

Third, we want someone with the ability to understand, for "wise words come from the lips of people with understanding" (Proverbs 10:13). Understanding comes with discernment and discernment comes from listening. Wise counselors are slow to speak for they are focusing on listening in order to understand. Many times, the obvious problem will not yield to a solution because the real problem hasn't been identified yet. It is interesting what can happen when someone listens to us with understanding. As they see beyond the obvious, they help us discover the possible resolution.

Someone Who Will Keep a Confidence

Fourth, we want to turn to someone we can trust, someone who will not discuss our problem with others. Solomon says, "A gossip goes around revealing secrets, but those who are trustworthy can keep a confidence" (Proverbs 11:13). So often, the person with the problem finds the pain com-pounded by the insensitivity of someone he or she trusted, someone who found a way to gossip about the situation. And making it a prayer request is still gossip. We need someone who will keep a confidence.

Someone Who Won't Intensify Our Pain

Sometimes, the friend we turn to has met all the requirements suggested by Solomon. Unfortunately, our problem taps into some painful place within them and their response inflames our own anger, or intensifies our hurt. For example, Sarah called a friend whom she thought had shown wisdom over the course of their friendship and could be trusted. This friend had gone through a marital breakup that seemed in some ways similar to hers. She arranged to meet her friend for dinner.

As Sarah shared some of what had happened in her marriage that led to Gary leaving, her friend listened sympa-thetically. But when Sarah mentioned pornography, her friend almost choked on her coffee. She became enraged at Gary's behavior and started to tell Sarah all the things she needed to do to protect herself from him.

What Sarah didn't know—and no one really knew—was that her friend's ex-husband had also been addicted to pornography. For several months after they had separated, she had had new revelations about the extent of his involve-ment in that seamy behavior. Until this evening, she had been too embarrassed to tell anyone that side of their marital breakup. Now all of her pent-up rage came out and fed Sarah's pain so that she became even more angry with Gary. By the time the dinner was over, Sarah and her friend were ready to start a crusade to wipe out husbands involved in pornography.

Both Sarah's and her friend's pain were too raw for them to help anyone else. They had some important healing of their own to tend to before that could be a possibility. By the time Sarah got home, she was so worked up that it was hours before she could get to sleep. The behavior of her friend's ex-husband got mixed in with Gary's behavior, and her anger and hurt overwhelmed her. After she made a middle-of-the-night call to another friend, she finally calmed down and got a few hours of sleep. Wise counselors don't mix their issues in with your issues.

Someone Who Won't Use Religious Clichés With Us

When looking for counsel, we should avoid people who use spiritual clichés. They appear to be wise and godly, but both their wisdom and their godliness exist only on the surface. Job's three friends were this type of counselor. At first, they seemed to be wise. For seven days they simply sat with Job and were silent. They were overwhelmed with Job's misfortune and spent time just being with Job. But then they started trying to help.

They spoke when they didn't know what to say. They probably did this because they didn't know what to do. Beginning in Job 4, each of his three friends tries to help Job see that since he is suffering, he must have some hidden sin in his life. Perhaps he wasn't trusting God enough, or there was something he needed to confess. Here are Elphaz's opening words:

In the past you have encouraged many a troubled soul to trust in God; you have supported those who were weak. Your words have strengthened the fallen; you steadied those who wavered. But now when trouble strikes, you faint and are broken. Does your reverence for God give you no confidence? Shouldn't you believe that God will care for those who are upright?

Stop and think! Does the innocent person perish? When has the upright person been destroyed? My experience shows that those who plant trouble and cultivate evil will harvest the same.

JOB 4:3-8

And those are just the opening lines. It goes downhill from there as each attempts to convince Job that his problem is spiritual. When Job protests his innocence, the three friends speak even more directly to Job about his apparent blindness to his sin (see Job 15–20). Job responds to one by saying,

I have heard all this before. What miserable comforters you are! Won't you ever stop your flow of foolish words? What have I said that makes you speak so endlessly? I could say the same things if you were in my place. I could spout off my criticisms against you and shake my head at you. But that's not what I would do. I would speak in a way that helps you. I would try to take away your grief.

JOB 16:2-5

It is interesting to note that at the end of the Book of Job, God doesn't rebuke Job for his questioning, or for arguing with

God. Instead, God rebukes Job's three friends for their inane, wrongly stated, spiritual arguments. He says to one of them, "I am angry with you and with your two friends, for you have not been right in what you said about me, as my servant Job was.... My servant Job will pray for you, and I will accept his prayer on your behalf. I will not treat you as you deserve, for you have not been right in what you said about me, as my servant Job was" (Job 42:7-8).

People who use clichés in their efforts to help are no more effective than those who use common sense as a guide. They are both overly simplistic and deal only with the obvious. They will never get to the root of the issue. It seems that the only one helped by the cliché is the person offering it, for they have the satisfaction of trying to help. Some of the common religious clichés include, "You need to just trust God more"; "Have you prayed about this?"; and "Have you been keeping your quiet time each day?" People who offer clichés never realize that they are like Job's friends—operating in an attitude of judgment, not compassion.

How to Find Mature, Godly, Wise Friends

Here are three principles to help you find wise counsel from a friend.

First, look for someone who's been where you are and is now beyond where you are. That means they have been through the deep water but have found dry land. Sarah thought she had done this with the friend she invited to dinner. Her experience that evening made her gun-shy about sharing with anyone else. The big question for her was, "How do I know they are beyond their own issue?"

Here's what a friend suggested to Sarah after she described her horrible evening. What she ought to do in the future was spend time asking the other person about her own experience. Frequently we hurt so badly that we simply want to tell someone else about our suffering. That was how Sarah felt that evening at dinner. She thought she had found someone who would understand the incredible pain she experienced over Gary. In her pain, she started telling every detail of what had happened.

If she had asked questions, and allowed her friend to share more of her own story, she might not have uncovered her friend's unresolved issues with her ex-husband's addiction to pornography. But a sense of mutuality could have developed between them. In fact, after listening to much of her friend's story, Sarah might have asked if pornography had been involved. Depending on her friend's response, she might have shared Gary's problem. It would depend on how secure she felt in the response of her friend.

Second, look for someone who is older. It's not always true that wisdom comes with age. But it is true that the development of wisdom does require age. Ty and Ellie had several peaceful months with the girls, and then their older daughter, Brittany, started to get moody, and her grades started to slide. They had resolved the problem with Ashley but they had been careful to do the same things with Brittany, partly because they didn't want the focus to be on Ashley as the family problem.

Now Ty and Ellie were puzzled. Where should they turn? One Sunday at church they sat next to an older couple they really liked. Sometime during the service, Ellie remembered that they had two grown daughters—perhaps she had noticed them in the choir. She wondered what this older couple had done with their girls when they were the ages of Brittany and Ashley. After the service ended, Ellie struck up a conversation with the couple. She asked if they could get together sometime to talk about parenting. The other couple agreed.

When she told Ty later on, he was pleased. He thought Ellie had hit on a great idea. Later that week when the two couples got together, Ty and Ellie shared what had been going on with their girls, and asked if the other couple, George and Mary, had ever had anything like that happen with their daughters. They both laughed, and then Mary proceeded to share situations that seemed all too familiar to Ty and Ellie. Three hours later, Ty and Ellie not only had George and Mary praying for their family, they had some new tools, and a renewed confidence as parents that what they were experiencing wasn't abnormal. Over the next couple of years, a close friendship developed between George and Mary and Ty and Ellie.

Anne decided that candidly talking with her friend about her job situation was still too threatening. And she had put most of her faith questions on hold for now in order to try to feel more secure at work. She thought of talking with one of the older employees who were on the same level as her boss, but never had the opportunity. The process was slow, but the feelings of panic she experienced earlier had calmed down.

Third, it is important not to give up. Sarah needed to try again. A bad reaction from one friend doesn't mean there is no one who can be supportive. Ty and Ellie realized it was time to take things a step further and ask someone for help. What they had accomplished earlier was good, and they could build on that now that there were new problems to deal with.

And Scott hadn't given up yet; he was just waiting for the right opportunity. He needed to talk with someone not only about his issue at work, but also about his faith issues.

Marianne, on the other hand, hadn't tried any of these avenues of help. She felt her situation was beyond any book, tape, or video and that there was no one who would really understand what was going on in her home. This was complicated by Scott's behavior when he was out in public. Out there, he acted like everything was OK. He wasn't going to tell anyone about his job problems or how he acted at home. He really didn't think there was a problem. On the church softball team, he was not only one of the best players; he was fun to be around. Everyone enjoyed Scott. Marianne felt trapped with nowhere to turn.

Obviously, Marianne needed more help than even a wise friend could offer. She needed to talk with someone who might have some influence on Scott. When she saw the pastor at one of the games, she made an appointment with him. Maybe he would be able to help. In Marianne's case, her search led her to a different type of wise counsel—a spiritual mentor. Let's look now at the role of the pastor and of those in the church trained to be peer counselors.

Summary
The value of turning to a friend can best be utilized when

- we need supportive people around us to care for us and pray for us.
- we feel overwhelmed and have lost our perspective.
- the problem is not a repetitive pattern in our lives.

- the problem is related to a relatively recent event in our lives and is not a long-term, ongoing problem.
- we still have some hope for the future.

FIVE

Talking to Your Pastor or a Peer Counselor

Most of us will turn first to a friend, but the pastor is the person contacted more often than anyone else when friends can't help. Typically, we will talk with a friend or two, and then when that doesn't provide relief, we will call the pastor. Sometimes we are not comfortable talking with friends about a particular problem, and the pastor usually seems the safest person to confide in.

This was how Marianne felt. She was certain that no one else would understand her situation with Scott. She tried to talk to her sister but she advised Marianne, "Get rid of the bum. I don't know how you've put up with him this long." Marianne thought that the only safe person she could talk with, the only one who shared her values regarding her marriage vows, was the man who married them. He also seemed older and wiser, and perhaps most importantly, she noticed that he treated his wife well. All of these factors made her feel safe in asking him for wise counsel. She called and made an appointment.

Marianne didn't tell Scott she was going to talk to Pastor Ray. She was afraid he would try to stop her, fearful that she would say negative things about him—a fairly valid fear. As she shared what had been going on, their pastor listened carefully and made comments at times to make sure he understood what Marianne was experiencing. When Marianne finished, he suggested they pray together. Pastor Ray then sat quietly for awhile before offering some suggestions.

First, he said that he would call Scott and arrange to meet with him. As an experienced pastor, Ray knew there were two sides to every story, and he wanted to hear what Scott had to say. Marianne was thrilled at this possibility, especially as Pastor Ray continued. He said he had two things he wanted to discuss with Scott: He wanted to talk about the condition of his soul. Was he born again? And he wanted to put Scott in touch with one of the men in the church who had recently retired from his position as a very successful CEO of a medium-sized company. This former CEO had successfully mentored young men and guided them in their careers. He asked Marianne to pray that Scott would be open when he came in for his visit. Marianne agreed, and she left feeling a renewed sense of hope for her marriage.

By the time she returned home, Pastor Ray had already called Scott and made arrangements for him to come in for a talk. Marianne was a little nervous about his reaction to her visit with their pastor, but Scott seemed happy about the call—especially since he knew Pastor Ray from the baseball games. And the pastor had apparently framed his request to Scott in a way that didn't create a problem between him and Marianne.

Obviously, Marianne had chosen a pastor with some good training in pastoral care and counseling. Not every pastor has this kind of shepherd's heart. Some pastors are more gifted as teachers and are very strong in the pulpit ministry. Other pastors are more gifted as evangelists, and their churches grow as people come to know the Lord. Other pastors may have a prophetic ministry, and speak out about the problems in our culture. While they each may be able to give wise counsel in certain situations, the variety of issues presented by Marianne made this a complex case. It drew on all Pastor Ray's training.

Scott went to see Pastor Ray the next day. Very quickly, the pastor made him feel comfortable, even as he shared some of the concerns Marianne had related to him the day before. He focused first on Scott's job situation. After talking about it with Scott for awhile, he suggested that he could arrange a meeting between Scott and Bill, the retired CEO. Scott was impressed that Pastor Ray would even think of doing this. No one had ever taken an interest in Scott's career. When Scott agreed, the pastor picked up the phone and arranged a time and place for Scott to meet Bill for lunch.

Then Pastor Ray said he wanted to ask Scott about something more personal, Scott's relationship with the Lord. Scott listened carefully and in the end said he was interested—he had been listening to the sermons on Sunday—but wasn't ready to make a commitment to Christ. As Scott's time with the pastor came to an end, Pastor Ray said he would check back with him after his lunch meeting with Bill. He also wanted to talk to both him and Marianne the following week. They set a tentative time, and Scott left feeling a renewed sense of hope.

Why We Seek Wise Counsel From a Pastor

Pastor Ray had developed some important skills for giving wise *counsel*—skills that our friends probably wouldn't possess:

- He dealt with the spiritual issues involved.
- He prioritized the problems and only dealt with two of the issues.

- As a result, there were concerns Marianne had that he didn't address.
- He showed his care and concern for both Marianne and Scott.
- He built credibility with Scott by helping him with career issues.
- In each situation, the person left him with a sense of hope, not despair. This might not always take place, but in the beginning, it is very important.
- He had access to other resources.

Let's look at each of these points more carefully.

Able to Work With the Spiritual Issues

We expect the pastor to be comfortable talking with us about spiritual things. We expect him to know what the Bible has to say about the problem we face. And we expect him to talk to us about that.

Anne finally had a talk with an older man at work about her job situation. He had given Anne good advice that she immediately implemented. As a result, she felt more secure in her job. Now she was more aware of her spiritual struggle with God and all the questions racing around in her mind. Finally, she decided to open up and talk with one of the pastors.

Anne chose a different type of pastor from the one Marianne chose. She wanted someone who was more like a teaching pastor or a prophetic pastor. One of the associate pastors at her church had always challenged Anne to think about her faith. She decided she would set up a meeting and share her struggle with that pastor. A part of Anne was still hesitant out of fear that the pastor might judge Anne as weak in her faith, or consider her questions stupid. But the anxiety she felt over not talking about her questions was greater than her anxiety about being judged by the pastor. So she made the call and set a meeting time.

After exchanging some pleasantries, and praying together, Anne shared with Pastor Dale the struggle she had at work and how that had challenged her understanding of her relationship with God. Pastor Dale listened carefully. He made some notes as she talked and then started to ask Anne questions not only about her faith, but about how she had come to know Jesus as Savior.

They spent two hours talking. Pastor Dale took Anne's questions very seriously, never making her feel stupid for asking them. He even shared some of the questions he had grappled with in the development of his walk with the Lord. Then the pastor took two books from his bookshelf and gave them to Anne. "Start reading one of these and then let's get together again next week and talk about any answers you may have found there, or any new questions you might have," he said. They prayed again as they ended their meeting, and Anne left feeling there were some answers out there, and that her questioning wasn't a sign of weakness or failure.

Able to Prioritize the Problems and Provide Focus
Just as Pastor Ray was able to pick out two issues among all the concerns that Marianne had shared, and to focus only on those two issues to begin the healing process, Sarah's pastor was able to help her the same way. Sarah noted that her church offered a six-week divorce recovery workshop. She

called first thing Monday morning to arrange a meeting with the pastor in charge of that. As she spilled all the pain of her broken marriage and the reality of Gary's sexual addiction, her pastor helped her see that she needed to separate those two issues and deal with them one at a time.

Sarah had been spinning out of control in her thoughts and emotions. She had many questions about Gary's addiction to pornography, and just as many about what she might do to mend the marriage. The more she wrestled with these two issues, the more they got mixed together and the more confused she became. Her pastor suggested that she put the sexual addiction issues aside temporarily and look first at the issues of her pending divorce. Gary had recently filed papers, asking for a divorce, and that had stirred up every possible emotion within Sarah.

They spent the rest of their time together talking about the divorce, and how Sarah was dealing with that. The pastor acknowledged the seriousness of Gary's sexual issues, but stayed focused on what Sarah was doing about the end of her marriage. He answered her questions about the biblical basis for divorce, and helped Sarah apply them to her particular situation. As they finished talking, he enrolled her in the workshop and told her he would see her there.

Able to Show Care for All Parties Involved

A pastor must provide for the care of each person's soul under him. We saw this very clearly in the case of Scott and Marianne. The pastor didn't align himself with Marianne against Scott, as a friend of Marianne's might do, even out of the best motivation. A wise pastor knows that he wants to be able to help everyone involved, not just the person sitting across from him.

The same was true in Sarah's situation. Perhaps no one on the church staff knew what had happened to her and Gary until she came for help. Sometimes we get lost in our church family, especially if it is large. But once the pastor knows what is going on, he might, and maybe even should, call the other parties involved to meet with them as well. Jude reminds us that not only pastors, but all of us are to "Show mercy to those whose faith is wavering. Rescue others by snatching them from the flames of judgment. There are still others to whom you need to show mercy, but be careful that you aren't contaminated by their sins" (Jude 22-23).

Able to Impart a Sense of Hope

You'll notice that each person left his or her session with the pastor strengthened by a sense of hope. A good pastoral counselor will impart this sense to those in distress because the gospel, after all, is a message of hope, of good news. And the God we serve is a God of redemption and hope. He takes the bad things that happen in our lives, and desires to redeem them—to turn them into something good and holy. Jeremiah writes, "'For I know the plans I have for you,' says the Lord. 'They are plans for good and not for disaster, to give you a future and a hope'" (Jeremiah 29:11). A pastor should be a messenger who proclaims that plan for good and who gives hope.

Able to Point Us to Other Resources

In each case we described in this chapter, the pastor pointed someone to another resource. Scott's pastor arranged a meeting between Scott and a retired CEO; Anne's pastor gave her several relevant books to read; and Sarah's signed her up to attend the divorce recovery workshop.

The pastor able to give wise counsel is usually aware of the resources available within his community. He is one of the primary gatekeepers of help for those who are hurting. If he can't help, he certainly knows who can. And as in many churches today, he may even have other caregivers linked to the congregation who have been trained to counsel. These people are commonly known as lay counselors, peer counselors, people helpers, or caregivers.

Pastor Ray had a fairly large group of people trained to assist in situations like Scott's. What Scott didn't know, and really didn't even need to know, was that Bill, the retired CEO, was one of these peer counselors who had been trained within the church family. So not only was Bill equipped to help Scott with his work-related issues, Bill could also get involved in some of Scott's other issues.

Finding Wise Counsel With Peer Counselors

What is a peer counselor? These are lay people, specially trained in counseling skills, who work under the supervision of a professional counselor. As early as 1968, researchers found that people helped by peer counselors do as well as or even better than people who have sought help from a professional counselor.[1] How does talking with a peer counselor differ from talking with a friend? The key is the training they have received.[2] Most peer counselors have been through an experiential course where they not only received the necessary knowledge, they also practiced how to be effective helpers. Once they complete the initial training, peer counselors are involved in ongoing supervision in order to refine their counseling skills.

When I've trained peer counselors, I've devoted much time and attention to good listening skills. A number of times, those in the class have said they never knew they had to work so hard just to listen to someone.

Churches that have trained and supervised peer counselors usually limit the number of people each counselor can work with at any point in time, and they limit the number of sessions a peer counselor can have with someone before referring them to a professional. When this type of program is effective, usually at least one of the pastoral staff is closely involved in leading the program.

What About a Life Coach?

One of the growing categories of people helpers are those who call themselves life coaches. This is a movement that started in sports, but soon worked its way into the world of business. There, managers and executives are coached on how to better use management skills and how to be more effective in business. Recently, the scope of coaching has expanded to all areas of life.

Gary Collins, in his book, *Christian Coaching*, says "coaching is the art and practice of guiding a person or group from where they are toward the greater competence and fulfillment that they desire."[3] He notes the similarity of coaching to mentoring and discipleship. It is different from counseling in that it typically does not look at the influences of the past, nor does it seek to repair personality issues. Rather than trying to fix a problem, it seeks to motivate a person toward the future and the goals they want to accomplish.

Among our case studies, Ty and Ellie have enlisted the help of an older couple to be mentors for them in their parenting. In some ways, the older couple serve as life coaches in the area of more effective parenting. The older executive at Anne's company could also be considered a coach, since he is providing a form of mentoring.

But Sarah doesn't need a life coach at this point. She has hurts and pain from past situations that need healing. At some point in the future, after Sarah has recovered from her divorce, and from the painful memory of her husband's unfaithfulness, she might want to work with a life-coach to discern a future direction for her life. We're not sure yet about Scott. At this point, he still needs lots of wise counsel.

The Limits of the Pastor or Peer Counselor

There are limitations inherent in each form of nonclinical counseling. For one thing, a pastor is restricted in the amount of time he can devote to counseling. Unless that is his defined role on the pastoral staff, he will need to limit the number of times he can meet with any one person or couple. Many pastors will meet for three to six sessions but after that, they will refer the person or couple to a peer counselor or to a professional counselor.

There was a time some years ago when a number of pastors tried to define their ministry as that of a counselor. They saw people in the church office every day of the week. Unfortunately, the rest of their ministry suffered and they burned out trying to do everything. That's why those who do counsel today usually limit the time they devote to that work.

Most every peer counseling program I am aware of also limits the number of times the peer counselor will meet with someone. In this situation, the limitation is not because of time constraints, for each peer counselor is only seeing one or two people at a time. The restriction is in place because there is a limit to the amount of help a peer counselor can give, and that help should occur within six to ten sessions. If the problem hasn't been resolved during that period, it most likely needs the attention of a professional counselor. Often this is determined in conference between the peer counselor and the professional overseer before the sessions run out.

It should also be stated clearly that both peer counselors and pastoral counselors, for the most part, have a limited number of skills. There are types of problems they have been taught to refer on to professionals. Typically these are the main criteria used for making a referral to a professional:

- The person seeking counsel has prolonged emotional distress.
- The person has difficulty responding appropriately to advice because of emotional factors.
- The person has a distorted perception of the situation, and the counselor cannot correct these distortions.
- The person has suicidal or homicidal thoughts or impulses.
- The person is engaging in actions harmful to themselves or to others, for example, self-mutilation, spouse abuse, or child abuse.
- The person is having difficulty functioning appropriately and meeting normal expectations and responsibilities with job or family.

Usually, the pastor or peer counselor will refer a person to a professional when they feel overwhelmed by the problems of the person they are counseling, or they feel lost or unable to deal with the problems being presented. A good pastoral or peer counselor will know when to refer people to a professional.

Summary

You should consider turning to your pastor or to a peer counselor when

- there is a spiritual component to your problem or struggle.
- you are struggling with feeling safe when you talk about your problem.
- you need someone who can see the bigger context of your problem.
- you are able, in spite of the problem, to respond to advice and suggestions and to make adaptive changes.
- you are having difficulty perceiving your situation accurately.
- you are not a danger to yourself or to others.
- you can still meet your responsibilities.

Part II

Clinical Helpers

SIX

Choosing a Professional Counselor

Finding the right professional is not always an easy task. If your pastor says to you, "I know just the person you need to see," then he has simplified your situation. But it usually isn't quite that easy. When someone asks me for a referral to a professional counselor, I don't always have a ready answer. If one of my sons said to me, "I'm thinking of seeing a professional counselor, who do you think I should see?" I would really have to do some research.

Eventually I would tell my son what I tell others. "Here are several names of people I am familiar with. But do your homework and check them out." Once we have moved into finding help from a clinical source, we will have to pay something for this help, and that makes us a consumer. As a consumer, I have the right to ask questions about the service I am going to receive. Here are some of the questions I suggest you ask, prior to your first appointment, if possible:

- What training have you received?
- What are your fees?
- What is your specialty?
- What approach would you begin with in addressing my problem?
- What makes your approach particularly Christian?

- Are you comfortable talking about your faith in a counseling session?
- How many sessions do you typically have with a person?

If someone is not willing to discuss your questions, think twice before making an appointment. Some counselors will meet with a person for a free consultation, but that is not everyone's policy. If they won't talk with you on the phone, and you have few other choices, ask if they will meet with you for a preliminary session. I know several counselors who will do this, and if the person chooses to continue with them, will charge them for that session. If there is no "fit" between the counselor and the person, there is no charge.

The Types of Professionals

Once I have made a decision to see a professional counselor, I have an additional problem: What type of counselor do I need to see? While some states have different names for various levels of counselors, here are the main categories of professionals and the differences among them.

Psychiatrists

Psychiatrists are medical doctors. They have "M.D." after their names and have all the qualifications of a general practice medical doctor. Because of this, they can prescribe medication just the same as any other medical doctor. After finishing their basic medical education, they specialized in psychiatry. This means they did an extra three years of training (sometimes more) in order to devote themselves to the field of mental health.

Some psychiatrists work only with severely mentally and emotionally ill people, and with their families. Many of these psychiatrists will work in a mental hospital, treating the long-term mentally ill. Other psychiatrists practice both in the hospital and in an office, and will see patients with a variety of emotional and mental problems, usually problems that need medication as part of the treatment. There are also psychiatrists who specialize in issues such as depression or bipolar disorder and who counsel people on a weekly or more frequent basis in their office.

Psychiatrists must pass state exams in medicine and then pass a series of exams in the field of psychiatry. Their license is given by the state and must be renewed at regular intervals. Most states require psychiatrists to pursue continuing education every year in order to renew their license. Because of their extensive training, their fees are usually the highest of those who offer counseling.

Psychologists

With very rare exceptions, a psychologist is someone who has a Ph.D., or a Psy.D., or even an Ed.D., after their name. They have completed doctoral level work and are legitimately called "doctor." After completing their bachelor's degree, they earned a master's degree followed by the doctoral degree. This typically amounts to four to six years or more of additional training after college, and will usually include a one-year internship at a clinical facility, such as a veterans' hospital.

Psychologists are not medical doctors and therefore are not

able to prescribe medication. However, this is slowly changing. A dentist is allowed by law to prescribe medications related to dental work. Similarly, there is a growing movement to allow psychologists to prescribe a limited type of medications as long as they have taken additional educational training. New Mexico, for example, has voted to allow psychologists who have specialized training to prescribe medications. They are strictly limited to medication related to the area of mental health.

Every state has laws requiring the licensure of a psychologist. To be licensed, a person must have completed their doctoral degree and served a certain number of hours counseling under the supervision of a licensed psychologist or psychiatrist. The supervised hours usually cover a period of two years. After accumulating the required number of hours, a person must pass both written and oral exams. Most states also require that psychologists take continuing education classes in order to renew their license.

Psychologists have a variety of specialties. Since they have a broad background in testing, some psychologists work in the area of assessments. They give tests to assess a person's abilities or disabilities. They counsel individuals, couples, or even families, depending on their interests and specialization. Because they have had long and extensive training, their fees are typically just a little below psychiatrist's fees.

Marriage, Family Therapists, Licensed Clinical Social Workers, and Licensed Psychological Counselors

These are better known as master's level counselors because many states require them to have a master's degree in order to be licensed. They do not need to have a doctoral degree but some continue on and receive the doctorate. Not every state has licensing requirements for this level counselor, although the number that don't is diminishing every year. The titles for a master's level counselor vary from state to state although the Licensed Clinical Social Worker (LCSW) is pretty much the same across the country. In California, a master's level counselor is called a Marriage, Family Therapist (MFT). Up until recently, the title was Marriage, Family, Child Counselor (MFCC). In Texas, many of these therapists are called Licensed Psychological Counselors (LPC's). The common thread through all of these licenses is that only a master's degree is required.

These counselors have usually completed a two-year graduate degree, followed by either two or three years of supervised experience before taking their state exams. In almost every case, a year of supervised training is considered to be fifteen hundred hours of experience under the direct supervision of a licensed supervisor. Even though their academic training is less than a psychologist or psychiatrist, all of them are required to have a certain number of continuing education classes in order to renew their state licenses.

Master's level counselors usually specialize in more relational or family related issues. While marriage is often a primary focus, many work with children. They use some testing in their counseling, but unless they have done additional study, their training isn't as extensive in this area as a psychologist's.

Pre-licensed Counselors
Both psychologists and master's level counselors go through what is sometimes called an internship. They are not considered

licensed at this time but are registered with the state, and follow all the rules that apply to licensed counselors. After completing their supervised hours, they are qualified to sit for the state exams. Their fees are usually lower because of their more limited experience, but they are working directly under the supervision of an experienced, licensed counselor. That counselor assists the intern in handling each case. The quality of the intern's work is often directly related to the quality and reputation of the supervisor's work.

Pastoral Counselors

There are also people who are not on the staff of a church but who work under the title of pastoral counselor. These are usually people who have been licensed in one state and moved to another; the state they now live in won't give them credit for their license. Sometimes they are required to do more schooling. But sometimes these people are ordained ministers and are allowed by the state to counsel under that title as long as they are part of a non-profit organization. They may charge fees for their service. Many of those who work this way in my area are well qualified and provide excellent counseling.

However, it is important to check the credentials of such counselors. Some people have been stripped of their licenses because of violating the law, or the ethics of the profession. When this happened, they simply changed their title to pastoral counselor and continued on counseling. If you are considering working with a pastoral counselor who is not connected directly to a church staff, be sure you ask about their training, any previous licenses they have held, and whether they have had problems that led to their losing their license.

Theoretical Approaches

We can better understand how a counselor works by making a simple distinction regarding theoretical approaches. To begin, we will divide all the professional counselors we have described into two broad categories. In one category, we have all the counselors who only work with individuals. Initially they may bring a couple in for counseling together, but then they refer one of the individuals to another counselor. They are only comfortable working with one other person in the room with them.

The other category includes all those who are comfortable working with more than one person in the room. They enjoy working with a couple or even an entire family. This is called conjoint therapy. These counselors can and sometimes do work with only an individual, but they prefer the interaction that comes when they work with more than one person.

Neither of these two categories is better than the other. They are simply two different styles. When you are choosing a counselor, and you want to see that counselor together with your spouse, you should find someone who enjoys working with two or more people at a time. If you want to work on something that is strictly personal to you, then you might look for counselors who spend most of their time working only with individuals.

Cognitive-behavioral

Let's make a brief overview of the various counseling theories. The first one is often called cog-b, an abbreviated form of cognitive-behavioral. Counselors who use this approach will focus primarily on the distorted thought patterns that are related to your problem. Professors in graduate school say people using this approach are "interpreting up," meaning they are taking your presenting problem and going up into your mind, especially into the thought patterns that reinforce your problem. In this approach, the counselor works very actively with you.

This is a very popular approach and is used in marital therapy and in treating stress, burnout, depression, anxiety, panic disorder, and other mood disorders. It is also the basic approach used in most short-term counseling and the one preferred by HMOs and managed care companies. It can be very effective in treating a wide range of emotional issues. People like this approach because it is very results-oriented. Usually the counseling moves very quickly with cog-b, but critics say the results aren't necessarily long-lasting.

Growth and Insight

Another common way for counselors to describe their theoretical orientation is to say they work on growth or insight. This style covers a number of theoretical approaches. The common thread is that the counselor tries to help people grow emotionally or have deeper insight into their problems so they can resolve them themselves. Techniques range all the way from the counselor restating what the client says in order to help the client better understand his problem, to having the client talk to an empty chair as a way to better understand his situation.

In this approach, the counselor is still quite active but less so than the cog-b counselor. This method is typically slower than cog-b, but those who use it say that because of a person's insight into the presenting problem, the results are more lasting.

Analytical Approaches

Analysis is the more traditional approach to counseling, and rather than interpreting up, we now interpret down—down into the depths of the soul and emotions. The counselor often looks at early life experiences that are being repeated in the problem situation.

Object Relations, for example, is such a theoretical approach. It looks at the quality of our early relationships within our family and how we continue to act out those patterns in our current relationships. There is a lot of support for this approach, but it takes much longer than the others and is usually very individually oriented in terms of the counseling. Critics say it is much too involved, but supporters feel that they are getting at the root of the problem so it doesn't resurface.

Family Systems Approaches

This is often the basic approach of those who like to work with more than one other person in the room. The family systems method may use parts of cog-b, of growth and insight counseling, and even of analytic counseling as part of its theoretical underpinning. However, it will always look at the individual problem in the larger context of family or other relationships.

According to this approach, those who are closest to us will resist any changes we may want to make, even positive changes. So any work we do in counseling must take into consideration these reactions and plan for them. Basically, the person is always considered in the larger context of his or her significant relationships, and any changes that are encouraged must take into account how these relationships will be affected by the change.

Each of these summaries has been very brief, but they give you the flavor of what to expect when you interview your potential professional counselor. In the next chapter we will look more closely at what each of these approaches entails.

Male or Female

When seeking a counselor you should consider whether you want to work with a male or a female counselor. In some situations, it won't make any difference as long as you can relate to and trust the person you are seeing. But in some cases you may want to think it through before you make the call. Here are questions to help you determine if the gender of your counselor is important:

- Is part of my problem the fact that I have a pattern of difficulty with men or women?
- Was my relationship with my mother or father conflicted while growing up?
- Is that relationship still conflicted today, or do I simply avoid relating to that parent?
- Am I dealing with something that would be embarrassing for me to talk about with the opposite sex?

Let's say that as a woman, you have been struggling in your relationships with men. Further, you had a very conflicted relationship with your father while growing up. As you consider these questions, you can see that a male counselor might possibly force you to face some of your unresolved issues with your father in the safety of a counseling situation. But you might also do just as well with a female counselor.

But let's modify that situation a bit. Let's say that you are also very embarrassed by something you have allowed a man to do to you recently. You've told no one about it and feel like you need to talk about it in counseling. Based on that added information, you would probably feel more comfortable and safer talking with a female. The choice is yours, but when you interview a counselor and they ask you what issues you want to deal with, they may have some suggestions regarding whether you would do better with a male or a female counselor.

Why Some People Avoid Professional Counselors

Let's be honest. There are some bad counselors out there who are licensed by their state. There are even some bad Christian counselors out there—I hope not where you live. These bad counselors have done things that only reinforce our fears about counseling, and consequently, some pastors and lay people will do anything they can to avoid seeing a professional counselor.

Fear

There is a false belief that a trained counselor can exert strange power over a person. Because counselors know so much about humans, some people fear that they can see right through a person, down to their darkest secrets. I've had people say to me, when they find out that I'm a psychologist, "Oh, I better be careful what I say, or you will know things about me I don't even know." I usually laugh. "Oh, don't worry," I assure them, "I don't work outside my office." But the truth is, I can't even do that in my office.

It's true that counselors can see patterns of behavior and understand motivations, but good Christian counselors will never invade the heart or mind of the person they are counseling. Our role is to be a consultant, or a facilitator who helps people break unhealthy patterns in their lives so they can live the life Jesus promised.

Others are afraid of counselors because they know someone who went to one and became very dependent upon that counselor. While there are a few unscrupulous counselors who enjoy fostering an unhealthy dependency, there are also very good Christian counselors who will utilize a healthy dependency with someone they are seeing. In this case, the dependency is a temporary effect that is part of the person's issues and part of the effective treatment.

I have worked with a pastor who had bad experiences with a Christian counselor and, as a result, warned people to stay away from counseling. For some reason we developed a friendship. As he got to know me and trust me, he referred someone to me. As he saw how I worked with this member of his church, he started to trust me and see the value of counseling again.

Often when someone is afraid of counseling, it is either because they know someone who had a bad experience, or because they really don't know what goes on in a counseling session. Building trust over time is part of counseling, and when done properly and effectively, there is really nothing to be afraid of.

Insurance Mentality

For some reason, we have an expectation in our country that anything related to our physical or mental health should be paid for by insurance. If our insurance won't pay for it, then we won't pursue it. Some people won't pay out of pocket for a procedure even if the problem is life-threatening. There is something wrong with this picture.

People usually pay for what they value. We are willing to spend large sums of money to buy a car. We don't expect someone else to pay for it. We spend money on our vacation. We don't expect some kind of vacation insurance to pay for it. If we want a new couch, we pay for it. In other words, we pay for what we value.

What if there are no Christian counselors on your insurance company's panel? What do you do? Do you forget about getting help? Do you see a non-Christian counselor? Or do you make the decision to pay for a good Christian counselor? Let's figure out the cost of seeing a good Christian counselor.

Let's say that the Christian counselor your pastor recommended charges eighty dollars a session. (Some charge much more, some charge less. The cost depends on location and training.) Let's say also that the counselor estimates it will take about six months of weekly meetings to work through your particular issue. That totals $2080 for counseling. Now let's put that in perspective. We'll assume that you are with an HMO and they will not pay anything. It's all up to you.

Make a list of all the things you might spend $2000 on over the course of the next year. Your vacation may cost more than that. What about the down payment on a new car? Couldn't you wait awhile on that? Are you going to spend that much on new clothes this next year? Now ask yourself what would happen if you made the $2,080 investment in yourself and your counseling. How would your life improve? Are you worth that kind of investment? I would hope so!

What if the $2,080 is beyond your means? How can you still get professional help? Your pastor probably knows of several Christian counseling centers that provide help with fees according to a sliding scale. The scale is usually based on your gross income and can be as low as $10 a session. You may have to see a counselor who is not as experienced, but they are usually supervised by an experienced, licensed counselor, giving you the benefit of the licensed counselor's expertise.

As I have already pointed out, in most states, a person in training for becoming a professionally licensed counselor must work for a period of time under the direct supervision of a licensed counselor. Clinics will often use these counselors-in-training to provide service for low fees. These counselors-in-training discuss their cases with their licensed supervisor, so you receive good quality counseling for a low fee.

Some churches do not charge for the services of professional licensed counselors on their staff. Other churches will help subsidize the counseling fees from their deacon's fund. There are also full fee counselors, who, as part of their commitment to ministry, will see a certain number of people a week at reduced rates. Don't hesitate to ask about this when interviewing various counselors.

Don't let the cost of professional counseling deter you from getting the help you need. Time doesn't heal all wounds. While it heals some, usually the things we need to work through with a counselor do not improve on their own. We need to make the investment, or seek help in making the investment, so that we can break the pattern that is causing pain and live more of the abundant life Jesus promised.

Finally, if you are still hesitant, talk with someone who has had a good experience in counseling. Your pastor may know of such a person who would be willing to talk with you. Or read the next chapter so you can better understand what happens in counseling and how it can help you.

Summary

You should consider seeing a professional counselor when

- your pastor suggests you do so.
- talking with friends, and even with a peer counselor, hasn't helped.
- you have found it nearly impossible to follow what's been suggested to you by others.
- there has been a long-term struggle with similar problems.
- it seems like no one really understands what you are struggling with.
- you struggle with feelings of suicide, or even of homicide, and they are starting to scare you.

- you feel like hurting yourself, or hurting someone else.
- your anger is out of control, and you are saying and doing things that are "not you."
- you are beginning to struggle with just doing the basic things you need to do for yourself, your family, or your job.

SEVEN

How to Work With a Counselor

Sarah decided to see a professional counselor. Her group leader in the divorce recovery workshop she attended had suggested that counseling might help. Now that the appointment was near, however, Sarah was filled with questions. What should she expect? What should she do in the counseling sessions to derive the most benefit from the experience? Where should she begin? Why should she have to pay for these sessions? How often should she meet with the counselor? How many sessions would it take before she felt better? Sarah had interviewed three counselors before choosing the one she felt was best able to help her. But now that the appointment time was here, these questions and others raced through her mind. Sarah's concerns are not uncommon—perhaps the same questions have occurred to you. A look at the various elements of counseling should provide some answers. We'll start with foundational issues and then look at the process of what actually happens during the sessions.

Two Foundational Questions Related to
Working With a Counselor

The answers to two basic questions can help us establish a good foundation for working with a counselor. Our first question is, What makes counseling work? Second, Apart from the fact that professional counselors have training, what are we paying for?

What Makes Counseling Work?

In asking this question, we are not looking at the theoretical base from which the counselor works. We want to look at something more universal. A wide variety of counseling styles has proven effective in helping people, even though these approaches are based on theories that often conflict. How could counselors work from conflicting points of view and still be effective? This reality was especially puzzling for students training to be counselors as they wrestled with which theoretical approach was the right one. Professors who were honest said that they all seemed to work; students had to chose a theoretical base to work from that was comfortable for them.

But then the question arises, Why do they all seem to work? What is their common denominator? It certainly isn't theory. The only answer seems to be connected to the relationship the counselor builds with the person seeking help. In other words, it is the counseling relationship—between counselor and counselee—that is most important for the success of counseling.

Most professional counselors, when pressed for an answer, would agree. Why is this true? What happens between the counselor and the counselee that is universal? Think about the four case studies we have followed in this book. What is a common issue among all of them? It is the issue of trust. Look at Ty and Ellie. They went to the bookstore first, where they could objectively evaluate the available resources. When they decided to talk with the older couple, it was because they felt they could trust them. They could be vulnerable in describing their problem because they felt the older couple would understand. They took the risk to see if trust could be built between them.

Anne struggled with the question, "Whom can I trust to talk with about my job and faith concerns?" Marianne was asking the same about her marital problems. And underneath the turmoil in Sarah's mind was the basic question, "Am I going to be able to trust this counselor enough to talk about the deeper issues in my heart?" And if either Scott or Gary were ever to see a counselor, their ability to trust that person enough to open up to them would be a major issue.

Trust is really the basic foundation for our development as persons. When we were born, we each came from the womb, a very safe environment. Our needs had been met before we even experienced them. We were never hungry, never malnourished, never too warm or too cold, nothing was loud or bright, and we had this wonderful symbiotic relationship with our mother through the umbilical cord. Then birth occurred and all that came to an end. We were alone in the universe for the first time. We experienced hunger, cold, loud sounds, bright lights, and burning diapers. Life was no longer safe, unless we were able to rebuild that close, warm relationship with the mothering person. She could make it feel safe again, but we would have to learn to trust that she would be there for us.

No mother can do this perfectly, for much of what makes the world safe for the infant is based on the infant's experience, and babies cannot tell us what that experience is. They can't tell us what they need. So there will be gaps, and our ability to trust will be damaged to some degree.[1] Perhaps if we lived in a sinless world, this wouldn't be true, but since "all have sinned" (Romans 3:23), we will all have some difficulty in experiencing a trusting relationship.

When we have deficits in our ability to trust as an infant, these are usually carried over into our adult relationships. We will have some good relationships that will help us learn to trust more, but we will also have hurtful relationships that will further damage our ability to trust. One of the unspoken tasks we often face when meeting with a counselor is to learn how to trust by learning to trust the counselor.

As Sarah begins her session, she will be doing a number of things and talking about a number of issues, but underneath all of that, she is going to be asking herself whether or not this person is someone she can learn to trust. And it is this trusting relationship that makes counseling work, regardless of the theoretical base the counselor uses.

What Are We Paying For?

The difference between the counseling we experience with a friend or with our pastor is that we are now talking to a professional counselor. They are professionals because they earn their living by the practice of counseling, and because they possess some kind of license or registration with the state. Since they earn their living by counseling, we know we, or we along with an insurance company, are going to pay for the counseling. We expect that. But what are we paying for beyond the fact that they possess a license and have been trained professionally?

I'm often asked this question and my answer is always, "You are paying for 'trustworthiness.'" If everyone were trustworthy, then we would probably not need very many professional counselors, as there would be a large number of people we could turn to for help. But that isn't the case. Trustworthiness is going to be an issue in any relationship. So licensure by the state not only means that a person has met certain training requirements and professional requirements, it also means that the counselor has agreed to work with other people in an ethical and professional way. Unfortunately, not every counselor maintains that agreement and there are those who lose their license from the state because of unethical behavior. But the fact that the state fulfills that function helps us to expect the person we are seeing to be ethical and trustworthy.

Ethical standards involve several issues. First, there cannot be any type of sexual relationship between the counselor and the counselee on any occasion whatever. Every professional organization and every licensing board agree on this point. Sex is never a part of counseling. When this occurs, and it is reported to the licensing board, the counselor will not only lose his or her counseling license, they may also face criminal charges. This is an absolute.

Second, the ethical guidelines are very clear about confidentiality. In fact, you as the counselee are the holder of confidentiality. A licensed, professional counselor cannot talk to anyone else about what you are working on in counseling, unless you give written permission. There are some very specific exceptions. Confidentiality can be broken if the counselor has reason to believe you are a threat to commit suicide, or that you are a threat to harm someone else. And confidentiality can be broken if the counselor has reason to believe there is child abuse or elder abuse taking place. The specifics of these exceptions to confidentiality should be clearly spelled out by the professional counselor at the beginning of your meeting together.

A third area spelled out in the ethical guidelines involves what are known as dual relationships. This means it is unethical for a counselor to relate with you in any way other than as a counselor. They cannot enter into a business project with you, have dinner with you, join your investment club, or develop any other kind of relationship with you that would allow them to take advantage of you in some way.

Sometimes the guidelines regarding a dual relationship are interpreted so strictly that a counselor may even feel uncomfortable seeing you in the grocery store, or attending the same church as you, since such occasions might indicate a dual relationship. But if you live in a small town, it may be impossible to avoid these types of contacts. And they don't really fit the description of a dual relationship in the way the ethical guidelines intend. I sometimes run into people I am counseling at church or at the store, and I tell them in advance that if that happens, I won't initiate a conversation with them. Since they are the holder of confidentiality, they have a choice as to whether they want to acknowledge me or not. They can decide what they are comfortable doing. If they don't want to speak with me, I won't even acknowledge that I know them.

Everything related to the law and ethics of how a counselor

works is there to make it safe for the counselee, and to help the counselee build a sense of trustworthiness in the counselor. When this takes place properly, the counselee is able to more effectively build trust in the ongoing relationship with the counselor.

The Process of the Counseling Sessions

Let's look now at what happens when we start meeting with a professional counselor. We'll divide the process into three segments: assessment, intervention, and termination.

Assessment

The first thing that will take place is an assessment of the problem. This will involve the counselor taking a detailed history of you and of the problem. Your counselor will want to know about your background and the background of the problem. He may use a questionnaire, an interview process, or tests. Each counselor will have his or her own way of getting the background to your problem.

In addition, the counselor will want to know something about your medical history and whether or not you have had a physical exam recently. The counselor may request that you be checked over by your physician to make certain that your symptoms are not related to a physical illness. This is especially true in relation to some of the symptoms of depression.

This is one of the first things the professional counselor should do with Scott. His symptoms of lethargy, his relational problems at work, his lack of involvement with his family all could be related to a physical problem such as an underactive thyroid. Unless the possibility of a physical problem is ruled out, the counseling may be rendered ineffective and be extremely frustrating for everyone involved.

In the situation with Sarah, physical causes were ruled out since she had met with her medical doctor prior to her counseling appointment. And there were clear, external factors— her husband's infidelity and his abandoning her—that were at the root of her problems. At her first session, her counselor, a woman, asked questions about the history of her marriage, the family in which she grew up, and her parents' marriage. Some of the questions seemed unrelated to Sarah's situation, but she answered them honestly and figured they must have had some relevance or the counselor wouldn't have asked them.

Basically, her counselor was trying to get background to Sarah's current situation. She wanted to know about Gary's family background, too, and about his parents' marriage because these were all influences in the kind of marriage Gary and Sarah built. Somewhere, there were weak links in those backgrounds that allowed the current problems to develop. Sarah can help her counselor by answering each question as thoughtfully as she can, even going back to add something that she thinks of later.

This may take more than one session, depending on the circumstances. But if you think of this assessment phase as giving the counselor a broad, detailed context in which to place your problem, you will be better able to see the relevance of each question.

Some counselors may begin this background interview on the phone when the appointment is made. And some counselors will want to give the counselee some psychological tests at the beginning to rule out certain issues, or discover more quickly some of the deeper issues that may be at work within the counselee.

At the end of Sarah's session, she stayed to take several tests. Her counselor explained that this was something she did with everyone she worked with, and that it helped get to the crux of the matter more efficiently. (Another counselor might have chosen not to give any tests, preferring to get all necessary information from the interview. There are advantages to either approach.)

When Sarah came for her second session, the counselor had scored the tests. Taking that information, along with the information she had received in the initial interview, she had several more questions for Sarah before they were ready to move to the next phase of counseling. Later, as her counselor looked at the test results, and the information she received from the first two sessions, she was able to formulate a more complete understanding of Sarah's situation, and develop a plan for future sessions.

Let's say, for example, that Sarah's counselor sees that Sarah has strong dependency issues that developed early in her life. She was the oldest of four kids, and her father was a very angry man. There were many times when she was the one who had to help her mother deal with fallout from her father's outbursts. She had learned early to take care of others, as she was often the one who protected her younger siblings when Mom and Dad fought.

In addition, the counselor can see from Sarah's tests that she is overly responsible, fearful, perfectionistic, and quite passive in her relationships. After she has examined the test results, she talks with Sarah about some of the findings to better assess how she and Sarah understand the results. After the testing and the two sessions together, her counselor has a good understanding of how Sarah's issues played into Gary's problems. She also sees changes Sarah must make in order to better deal with Gary in the future, and to avoid a repeat of her past relationship with Gary.

As the counselor begins the third session, she shares what she believes Sarah needs to work on in the counseling. Obviously, Sarah needed to grieve the end of her marriage and her extreme hurt at Gary's betrayals. Sarah knew this part of the counseling agenda, as those were the issues that led her to see a counselor.

But now she was also aware of issues she thought were problems, but had been unable to put into words. She needed to learn how to trust her intuition in relationships, to more firmly and assertively express her needs, and perhaps most importantly, learn where her responsibilities ended and where the other person's responsibilities began. She needed help in setting limits, or boundaries, in her significant relationships.

What if Sarah didn't agree with some of the things her counselor was suggesting to her? Well, since she was rather passive—according to the counselor—it would be difficult for her to say this. But if she didn't agree, it would be very important for her to express her thoughts and feelings. Any hypo-thesis that a counselor comes up with is exactly that, a hypo-thesis. It is an informed guess as to where the counseling needs to go. But since this was Sarah's counseling, she needed to express her questions, assuming she had some. What if she wasn't aware of these until after the session? Then she would need to bring her concerns up at the beginning of the next session. But since she and her counselor agreed on the goals, the next phase began.

Intervention

We've already noted in the preceding chapter that different counselors work in different ways. Some will work toward problem solving, and so for them, the definition of the problem is very important. This is especially true when counseling must be limited to a specific number of sessions, usually due to the restraints of insurance. Other counselors who work in a time-limited way will try to retrain counselees in specific skills that will help them work better within the problem situation.

Other counselors will work toward helping their counselees develop insight into their problems so they can resolve the problems themselves. They use questions, or reflect back responses, that help people see what they are saying, and thus provide greater insight into the motivations of their behavior.

There are some counselors who will use a combination of these methods to help people grow stronger. Growth is their focus, so they will retrain, help counselees learn how to better problem-solve, and provide insight into their own personal process. Other counselors will seek to interpret present behaviors and relational patterns by looking at past relationships, especially those experienced when a young child.

Rather than providing specific guidelines for how a person can work with each type of counselor, let's look at the common factors that enable a person to benefit the most from counseling, regardless of the approach of the counselor. Here are

some "don'ts" that will help your counseling be more efficient
and effective.

Don't story-tell.

Up to a certain point, the counselor needs to understand the
events that are going on in your life. This is called story-telling.
It isn't counseling if all you do in your time together is review
what has happened in your life since your last meeting. When
a counselor allows this, he or she is either tired or lost and
doesn't know how to help you get on track. Or you are such a
talker that the counselor doesn't know how to get a word in
edgewise. Good counseling always looks beyond the story to
the underlying patterns, and then makes an intervention in
the pattern in order to bring about change. So resist the urge
to fill your counselor in on all the details of your life.

Don't be afraid to express how you feel about the counseling to your counselor.

I have some of my best sessions when people get frustrated, or
even angry with me for some reason or other. I remember one
woman who came into the session angry because during the
last appointment I had encouraged her to tell me what was
going on in her job. I didn't do anything but listen and she felt
it had been a waste. I agreed, and we went at it and had a great
session, due in large measure to her willingness to tell me how
she felt about what we had done.

One of the important things a competent counselor will do
is acknowledge when he or she has missed the mark. More
important, he or she will be able to handle and contain your
negative emotions, including, especially, your anger. If I as

your counselor cannot accept your anger, even when it is directed at me, you are not going to feel very safe with me, and you will have problems trusting me with that part of your experience. And that will limit my effectiveness in working with you.

Further, what you are learning to do with your counselor is what you need to learn to do with the other people in your life. Your counselor is supposed to be a safe person with whom you can test new skills that are still uncomfortable for you. But when you learn to talk more directly and more assertively with your counselor, you will find yourself doing the same thing with the clerk at the department store, with your kids, with your spouse, and even with your parents.

Don't talk to everyone else about your counseling.

Quite often, people will begin to confront uncomfortable aspects of their personality in the counseling process. In their discomfort, which is usually experienced as some type of anxiety, they will talk in detail to their spouse, or to their friends, about what is going on in the counseling. They get differing opinions regarding their experience and unknowingly reduce the effectiveness of the counseling.

We can talk about our counseling, but a good rule of thumb would be to discuss only those parts of the counseling where issues have been resolved, or are close to being resolved. When struggling with something taking place in the sessions, keep it to yourself for awhile so you can wrestle with it internally. If you don't agree with some aspect of the counseling, confront your counselor and work it through in the session.

Don't worry about becoming dependent on your counselor.

Many people are afraid of counseling because they know someone who became too dependent on their counselor. This can happen in the course of counseling and, as I said earlier, it isn't necessarily a bad thing. In fact, in some situations, it is part of the treatment. Here are two ways it can happen—one good and one bad. First the good.

Remember, one of the issues we all work on in counseling is that of trust. Many of us see a professional counselor because we have trouble trusting others with very much of ourselves—we are "loners" emotionally. Usually our difficulty in trusting others stems from emotionally detached relationships in our early experiences, in particular with our parents. In a manner of speaking, we need to go through a reparenting process with our counselor. This usually happens when we look at those early issues of trust, although it can happen in any good counseling.

But this type of dependency is good because it indicates our growing ability to trust someone with vulnerable parts of ourselves. We are close enough, and feel safe enough, to look at areas of ourselves that even we avoided before we started counseling. When we work with competent counselors, they will talk with us about our growing feelings of dependency, and help us work beyond that dependency to a healthy sense of interdependence with them and with other people in our lives. The dependency is a temporary part of effective counseling.

When is dependency bad? You'll notice we used the word competent in regard to our counselor. Not every professional counselor is competent in this area. There are some people who are professional counselors because of unfinished issues in their own lives. Often these issues revolve around dependency— they have a need fulfilled within them when other people are dependent upon them. In their counseling, they foster a dependency that isn't part of the healing process for the counselee. It is for the benefit of the counselor. This is bad, not only because it prolongs the counseling, but also because the issue of dependency is never successfully addressed for the counselee.

How can you tell the difference? It isn't easy, and the incompetent counselor may be very good at convincing you that what is in fact an unhealthy dependency is normal and part of the treatment. Instead of fearing this issue, here are two things you can watch for that will keep you on track. First, know that a healthy dependency in counseling is always moving toward interdependence, which is a connected form of independence. Our healthy independence is best expressed and experienced in the context of connected relationships. And our experience of dependency has as its goal our experience of healthy independence.

Second, don't listen to your family and friends right away. Assume that they are being alarmist, in part because they have always seen you as independent. They are alarmed that you are different. However, when they start to express concern that your dependency has gotten out of hand, and can give you valid examples of how you appear to be stuck at this stage, listen to them. Make it an issue with your counselor. And as you make it an issue with your counselor, talk about what is being done within the counseling to help you move beyond dependency to healthy independence. Remember, you are the consumer. You are paying the bill. Therefore, you are in charge of your treatment.

Don't limit the goals of your counseling.

Often we go to a counselor to resolve a specific problem. But we also can see the counseling experience as an opportunity to learn new skills, new more effective behaviors, and to become a more balanced person. Our true objective is to live life as Jesus wants us to live it, "life in all its fullness" (John 10:10). The training and the objectivity of a professional counselor can help me see my blind spots. This will enable me to resolve the problem that brought me to the counselor and to learn things that will enrich my life.

Termination

Termination is not a pleasant word. Why couldn't we use a simple word like ending, or finishing? I don't know, I just know that professional counselors always talk about terminating the counseling. In a way that makes it easier to express the reality of what is happening: it's the counseling that is being terminated, not the healing and growth that counseling has initiated. This ending process needs to be seen as a part of the counseling process. All too often, as people begin to feel stronger and better able to deal with their problems, they just decide to stop coming to the counselor. They simply cancel the last session and don't reschedule. When they do this, they are missing an important part of the process.

Good counseling is always working toward an ending. But the ending needs to be discussed, just as the middle parts of the process needed to be discussed. When you, as the counselee, feel like you have reached a point where you can handle things on your own and don't need the help of the counselor, it is important to discuss this with the counselor. There is much to be gained by finishing.

I've had people call and cancel the next session, and say they are finished, only to have them call back several months later needing to resume the counseling. They had felt they were finished, but perhaps they were premature in their evaluation. Or they may have to come back because we didn't get to talk together about how to consolidate the gains they had made. Or they may have missed an important facet of the issues that, had we talked about it together, might have taken one more session to complete. Now it will take several sessions.

It's important to see that how something ends is as important as how it begins. It is not a case of a counselor trying to squeeze one more payment out of the counselee. Up to this point it has been a collaborative effort, and the ending needs to be collaborative as well.

Summary

In this chapter, we've looked at the process of counseling from the point of view of the counselee. One important consideration to add to our discussion is the question of how the counselor works collaboratively with the Holy Spirit in the counseling sessions. Some people feel much more comfortable when the counselor either begins or ends a session with prayer. Or they like it when the counselor will relate scripture to the topic being discussed. Some counselors only pray in the session when the counselee asks them to, but they pray daily for the people they work with daily. Any of these approaches indicates that the counseling process involves more than just the people in the room. It leans heavily on the power of God for its effectiveness.

I am always concerned when someone tells me that a Christian counselor either wouldn't give them a clear answer regarding whether the counselor would pray with them in the session or told them that praying together wasn't part of counseling. Obviously, some counselors are uncomfortable praying out loud with someone. If that is the case, and if prayer with the counselor is important to you, see someone else. This should be something you discuss with the counselor when you make your first appointment.

On the other hand, just because someone will pray with you or use scripture in the session, doesn't mean they are really working hand in hand with the Holy Spirit. Listen carefully to what they are telling you. Is it consistent with God's Word? Is their value system one that reflects an understanding of how a person's faith works itself out in daily living? Don't be afraid to discuss these issues, either at the beginning of the counseling or when something happens in a session that makes you wonder.

Another issue that bothers some Christians is the question of when and if medication should be a part of counseling. Let's look at that subject now.

EIGHT

Medications—Yes or No?

What do you do when your professional counselor suggests that you might need medication? Or what do you do when you watch a television commercial for a prescription drug that treats anxiety? As you watch, you say to yourself, "That's my problem—I wonder if those pills would help?" Increasingly, pharmaceutical companies are taking their product directly to the consumer, urging people to "ask your doctor about...."

For some reason, we have a different response to a commercial about a pill to lower cholesterol as opposed to a commercial about medication that lowers our social anxiety. This same differentiation is apparent when we take medication. If I'm on an antibiotic or blood pressure medicine, I'm not ashamed to tell you what I'm taking. But if I'm on an antidepressant, I now have a secret that I will share with very few people.

Unfortunately, there is still a stigma attached to what are known as psychotropic medications. These are the class of drugs that target emotional or mental problems, ranging from anxiety to severe mental illnesses such as schizophrenia. Frequently, people taking these drugs are unfairly judged as mentally ill, mentally weak, or lacking faith.

Some of this attitude may be based on old beliefs. Years ago there were a limited number of psychotropic drugs available, and those were only used for the most severe mental disorders. Today, the market is flooded with all kinds of medications, including very specific ones for depression.

This negative attitude is also based on the centuries-old philosophical distinction between the mind and the body. René Descartes, the seventeenth-century French philosopher, was particularly influential in promoting the idea that the mind and body are radically separate entities. His ideas advanced the development of today's medical science, but in the process we lost the sense of the interconnectedness of the body and the mind. Only recently has medical research focused again on the interaction of mind and body; popular attitudes, however, still see them as disconnected. Medical researchers no longer ask whether or not the body and mind are interconnected; they ask how many of our physical ailments have a causative mental or emotional factor. In other words, they are investigating whether some deadly diseases originate in the mind and the emotions; the results suggest at least 80 percent or more are interrelated. Even so, our attitudes about the role of mental and emotional factors in disease lag far behind the research.

In short, we are comfortable with the need to take insulin for diabetes, for example, or antibiotics for bacterial diseases, or medication to lower cholesterol. We may not like taking these drugs, but we do so, and talk freely about it. We are comfortable both taking and talking about these medications because we are treating a physical problem, not an emotional or mental one.

Our Fears Related to the Emotional Realm

Our reluctance to discuss our emotional problems leads not only to fear of talking about psychotropic medications, but also to fear of taking them when prescribed. In spite of the incredible advances that have been made in the effectiveness of these drugs, we still resist them, even when we know they will bring relief. Researchers have noted that many people who receive prescriptions from their medical doctor never get the prescription filled. There are many reasons for this aversion beyond the stigma we have already discussed.

Side effects, for example, are a major concern. Many of the older forms of antidepressants were accompanied by unpleasant side effects such as a dry mouth which, though not as unpleasant as the depression, was still frustrating. The new, so-called designer antidepressants have not only eliminated dry mouth, they have also eliminated most side effects for most people.

Cost is also a prohibitive factor. If medication is prescribed for a physical condition, we will buy it even if we struggle with the cost. But if it is prescribed for an emotional condition, we consider the expense optional. Or we may start the medication but become impatient waiting to see a change in our mood (the new antidepressants take awhile to become effective). Discouraged, we decide to save our money and not refill the prescription.

Many people fear that they will become habituated, or addicted to the medication. There are some psychotropic drugs that can be addictive, such as Valium or Xanax, so one must be careful to follow both the directions that come with the medicine and the advice of the physician. But most psychotropic medications are not addictive, physically or psychologically. Others fear some damage to the body, if not now then at a later date. And others would rather just tough it out, thinking that medicine is for the weak, especially since, alone, it doesn't address the real problem.

Christians have additional reasons they avoid medication. Some of the previously stated concerns are magnified within the Christian community. Not only are people weak if they take a psychotropic drug, the thinking goes, they also admit to a lack of faith and trust in God; they are spiritual failures. Taking medication is "an attempt to use a chemical to perform what the Holy Spirit should be doing in their lives, or silencing his [the Holy Spirit's] conviction in their lives because of unconfessed sin."[1]

Many of these concerns have some validity, and warrant a cautious approach to psychotropic medication. But there are many emotional problems that cannot be treated effectively unless the psychological pain is first reduced to some degree, freeing the person to work on the issue. It is similar to using a cast on a broken leg. A person may tough it out and refuse a cast, against medical advice, and the leg will eventually heal. But the refusal to use a cast will at best complicate the healing process, or at worst, compromise it.

The cast isn't the solution to the problem: a person doesn't wear the cast the rest of his life. The cast assists the process of proper healing, allowing the person to move around without reinjuring the leg and to resume normal activities. The cast provides the support that promotes effective healing of the real problem. In the same way, antidepressants provide the support that allows people to work more effectively on the roots of depression and to experience healing.

Sometimes medicine must be taken for a long period or even a lifetime. It depends on the purpose of the medication.

For example, someone who is bipolar—what used to be called manic-depressive—suffers from a biochemical problem within the cells of the body. Bipolar disorder is not just an emotional issue. Several drugs effectively treat the mood swings typical of this problem and provide stability in a person's life. Just as a diabetic takes insulin for a lifetime, the bipolar individual will take medicine for the rest of his life, unless some new, more effective treatment is discovered.

Why Take Psychotropic Medications?

The manner in which psychotropic medications work is directly related to why they work. For example, we are sometimes frustrated with our medical doctor because we want him to prescribe an antibiotic. But he says, "No, what you have is a virus, and we don't use an antibiotic to treat a virus. Your body has to fight that off." In the same way, there are emotional problems that will respond to medication, and there are others that won't.

Let's take depression as an example. Not every depression will respond to an antidepressant. Sometimes I am depressed because I have had a recent loss in my life. My depressed mood is an important part of my grieving, and as with a virus, I need to work my way through it. But there are types of depression that are more persistent and are rooted in a person's brain chemistry. Between the brain's countless nerve endings are "transmitter substances" such as serotonin, dopamine, and norepinephrine which influence a person's mood. In some depressions, these substances are depleted and, like a weak battery, respond slowly. We can increase our levels of serotonin or dopamine through activities such as exercise, but antidepressant medications are designed to increase these levels in different ways.

Some of the older tricyclic medications, such as Elavil or Tofranil, helped the body produce more norepinephrine, serotonin, and other transmitters. The newer anti-depressants such as Prozac, Zoloft, Paxil, Celexa, and Luvox are known as SSRIs—selective serotonin reuptake inhibitors—and operate on a different principle. When serotonin is released in the brain, passed from one nerve cell to the next, some of it is reabsorbed in the process. SSRIs block the reabsorption or reuptake of seratonin, increasing the supply of seratonin in the brain.

Some of these newer medications (such as Remeron) block a variety of transmitters. Others work on dopamine (Wellbutrin SR) and one works on both serotonin and norepinephrine (Effexor XR). When one of these medications is ineffective, the medical doctor will try one that has a different design, hoping it will work better. Research is ongoing in this area, and includes newer technologies using magnets (repetitive transcranial magnetic stimulation—rTMS) and surgical implants of pacemakers in the brain (vagus nerve stimulators).[2]

There are other antidepressant medications available today, and more will be available tomorrow as research continues. Each of these drugs works on the body's brain chemistry and, when prescribed properly and taken according to directions, is wonderfully ⸱ ⸱ The stigma and shame attached to taking these drugs will diminish over time as more people recognize their value in facing and working through certain problems.

How Are They to Be Taken?

These medications are not available over the counter, and are not appropriate for one person just because they have helped another. Here are some suggestions for how to make the best use of psychotropic medications, especially antidepressants. Dr. Michael Lyles suggests that there are "four Ds" to follow.[3]

Dosage

Unless the amount of medicine we take is within an effective treatment range, we may find that the medication doesn't work. This effective dosage is called the treatment level. If your medicine isn't working for you, ask your doctor to check your treatment level to see if you are taking the right amount. There are always variables regarding the correct dosage, including age, the presence of other medications, and our individual sensitivity to drugs.

Duration

Dr. Lyles points out that research suggests it may take six to eight weeks for some of these prescriptions to be fully effective. Twenty-five percent of patients respond to antidepressants in four to six weeks of therapy. Unless you are having side effects (and if you are, contact your physician immediately), don't give up. You might not have the desired response to the medication until you have been taking it for at least eight weeks.

Diagnosis

Sometimes medicine will not work because the diagnosis is wrong. And then there are some diagnoses that can only be confirmed through the person's response to the medicine. For example, this is true with bipolar disorder. Its diagnosis is based on a variety of elements, including the person's medical and emotional history, family history, and the presence of certain symptoms. But the diagnosis isn't confirmed until the treatment with a prescription (usually lithium or Depakote) is stable and effective.

The Correct Drug?

Based on the first three Ds, if a medication is indeed ineffective, other considerations must be taken into account. This is why, in certain cases, seeing a psychiatrist as opposed to the family doctor is especially important. When things aren't working ideally, the extensive training and background of the specialist—the psychiatrist—are important.

Summary

In order to feel more comfortable about taking psychotropic prescriptions, here are some things to keep in mind:

- *Don't be afraid.* As with any medicine, there are some risks. But these can be managed effectively by paying attention to your body's response to the medication, and checking with your doctor when something unexpected happens.

- *Use caution.* A psychotropic medication isn't a magic pill that will make everything better. There is an appropriate time to use this type of drug, and situations where it is not appropriate. Don't be afraid to bring your questions to your therapist and the prescribing medical doctor. You have the right to be informed about your medication.

- *Follow the doctor's instructions.* Don't medicate yourself. Do what the doctor told you to do. If you are having concerns about your reaction to a prescription, call the doctor right away. It is important to follow the directions when you start taking the medication, and equally important that you follow the directions when you stop. Some of these medications have what is known as a discontinuation syndrome. It is a characteristic of the drug, and does not mean you have become addicted. However, there is a way to stop taking them that will avoid a discontinuation response.

- *Don't stop just because you feel better.* Some people, when they feel better for awhile, stop taking their medication. This is dangerous because of the possibility of a relapse into the old pattern. In the case of depression, a relapse can prolong treatment and increase the chance of another relapse. Stay in treatment—both therapy and medication—long enough to prevent relapse.

- *Don't just use medications; get into counseling as well.* Taking medication for depression will certainly be effective, but treatment is most effective when medicine is combined with therapy. The best chance for healing occurs when people work on the deeper issues that caused the depression in the first place. Studies show that if the problem responds to medication, then medication by itself can be an effective treatment. Counseling by itself is also effective. In many situations, however, the most effective response has been a combination of both medication and counseling.

NINE

Finding Help in a Group

Sarah is coping relatively well with her pending divorce. Counseling helped, but the divorce recovery workshop she attended probably helped the most. The workshop lasted six weeks, and half of each session was spent in a small group led by a facilitator. Each week, the same people met in the same small group to discuss what the speaker had said, and to encourage each other.

Sarah hit it off with another woman in the group and they met several times for dinner. Their stories were different but their pain was similar; their new friendship became a stable point in their lives. In addition, Sarah looked forward to seeing the other people in the group each week. When the workshop ended, they had all agreed to keep meeting for mutual support.

Scott's counselor sent him to his medical doctor for a complete exam in order to rule out any physical problems related to his behaviors. That doctor had recommended Scott start a course of antidepressant medication. After several weeks, both Marianne and the counselor started to see some changes in Scott's behavior. He became more involved with his children, and even offered to help Marianne several times. Based on these small changes, his counselor suggested that Scott might benefit more from a therapy group the counselor led than from individual counseling. Scott agreed.

His counselor's group was quite different from Sarah's support group. The people in this group all seemed to have difficulty relating to each other, and much of what they worked on together were relational skills. They discussed what might have caused each of them to experience such a deficit in their lives. Sometimes the counselor focused on one of the group members. At that first meeting, Scott watched in fear that the counselor would focus on him. He finally did when Scott said something to one of the other group members and the counselor picked up on it. As they talked, Scott struggled to understand his own history. Others in the group showed concern, and shared aspects of their struggles that were similar. When the group ended that night, Scott felt a sense of relief as well as a feeling of excitement over some important insights he had gained. He didn't want to go through this every week, but he was relieved to find out that it wasn't so bad.

Two Types of Groups

Sarah and Scott are both in a group, but each group is quite different from the other. One is a support group; the other is a therapy group. These are basically the two types of groups available to us. Let's look at the characteristics of each.

Support Groups
Leadership of the group provides the most obvious distinction between these two types. A professional counselor will lead a

therapy group; a layperson—or a rotating roster of lay people—will lead a support group. A few support groups will have a professional counselor as a facilitator, but they are the exception, not the rule.

Some support groups are topical, such as Sarah's divorce recovery group. But as the group continues to meet together, the original topic that brought them together will fade, and they will focus more on supporting each other. Alcoholics Anonymous, Overcomers Outreach, and a tough-love parents group are other examples of topical support groups.

Many support groups are just that—a supportive group of people who meet together regularly. That would include some Bible study groups. My wife and I are in a couples' Bible study group that spends some time studying together, but part of our purpose is to be a support system to each other. Covenant groups or accountability groups are also examples of support groups.

There may be an informal agenda in a support group, but what usually happens is that at some point during the meeting, people share what is going on in their lives. Sometimes the others in the group provide helpful insights; other times, they simply listen. Christian support groups usually have a time where members pray for each other as they seek to build an intimate community of people who care about each other.

A support group works best when there are at least three people, and no more than fifteen. Eight is the optimal number. If the group becomes too large, the sense of personal support is lost and individuals fade into the woodwork. It is easier to get to know each other in a group of around eight people; also, it is almost impossible to avoid participating without group members' noticing.

Sarah's workshop had several hundred people attending. If they only met in the large group, it would have simply been a workshop; anything personally supportive would have occured randomly, if at all. But the leaders wisely divided the large group into small units of eight to ten people, plus a facilitator. That way, everyone had the opportunity to participate, to get to know and support each other personally, and to build long-lasting friendships. The approach worked so well that the church held the workshop regularly.

Therapy Groups

Of course, there are similarities between these two types of groups. Both may be based on a topic, both can be time-limited or ongoing, both are subject to size limitations in order to be effective, and both aim to help people develop closer, more connected relationships. What is the difference between them, apart from the fact that a professional counselor is leading a therapy group and may be charging a fee for those who are participating?

One difference is the degree of intensity regarding what happens in the group. In Scott's group, described at the beginning of the chapter, the counselor focused more deliberately on the different individuals in the group. Because a professional is leading the group, personal issues can be pursued in greater depth. In Scott's case, he needed to connect his current problems—such as his issues with bosses and work—with deeper patterns in his life, particularly his experiences growing up. Let's look at what might happen to Scott in a therapy group.

As the group becomes aware of Scott's tendency to sit back

and watch, someone in the group confronts him about this. At first, Scott is defensive, just as he is whenever Marianne confronts him. He tends to blame other people, and when that doesn't work, he becomes silent and withdrawn. The counselor asks Scott what is going on inside of him at this point: what is he thinking and feeling in the silence? No one speaks until Scott finally starts talking. He says he learned to sit silently because as a child, if he did anything else, his raging father would punish him. He learned early to avoid being noticed as a way to avoid his father's verbal and physical abuse.

The counselor had the skills to keep Scott talking, even when Scott started to fight back tears. For perhaps the first time in his memory, Scott was talking about a very painful part of his past that plagued him in the present. He reported that several times he had been fired when, after tolerating an abusive boss, he finally blew. "How come I keep getting bosses that treat me like my dad did?" he asked at one point.

What went on during the time the group focused on Scott was similar to what might have gone on in a private counseling session. But in the group, others made comments, not just the counselor. Some shared empathically with Scott, having had similar experiences. Others commented on what they saw in Scott that was different from what Scott assumed his father saw in him.

When the group ended that night, Scott felt emotionally and physically drained. In a support group, people usually leave a meeting feeling supported and encouraged by the others. Scott's experience in the therapy group exhausted him. He had explored a deep part of himself that had lain hidden for years; it had been hard work uncovering it. He was grateful to the others who had helped him in that process, and he felt their support, but that wasn't his primary experience of the group that night.

In the midst of his tiredness, Scott also felt a glimmer of hope. Marianne felt it also as she listened to Scott relate what he had explored that evening. There was still a lot of work ahead for Scott, but he felt he had cracked open the door to his heart just a bit. It was scary in many ways, but he was beginning to feel safe in the group and looked forward to the next meeting.

The Value of a Group

A good group can be a powerful means of finding help, in part because of the variety of people involved. Over my years as a professional counselor, I have seen individuals grow and change at a faster rate and a deeper level than they would have working one-on-one with someone. The key seems to be that the work and healing is taking place in a larger context of relationships: If building a healthy relationship with one person is helpful, then building that same kind of healthy relationship with seven or eight people can be even more helpful. But apart from the relational aspect, here are three other reasons why a good group can work well.

1. *It is a safe place to test out new behaviors.*
Both Scott and Sarah were testing new behaviors in their group. Sarah was learning how to ask for support when she needed it, rather than waiting silently as she had with Gary. Now, when she is struggling with her hurt and pain, she calls one of these new friends. They feel safe to her because they

are going through much the same thing, and together they support each other.

Scott is learning to open up after being shut down for as long as he can remember. He doesn't share deeply every week, but over the past several months he has talked about a number of personal issues. That has led him to a greater level of openness and trust within the group. What he has been learning to do in the group, he has tried to do with Marianne. Most of the time, she has been very supportive as he has explored new ground with her in his life and his marriage.

2. *There are multiple people to give feedback.*
When I was in training as a professional counselor, I had to take a class on group therapy. The class was very experience-oriented; there was no lecture. Each time we met, some of us sat in a therapy group inside a room surrounded by one-way mirrors. I volunteered to be in this group.

I think I chose to be in the demonstration group not only to learn as much as I could, but also to look at some scary issues within myself. I waited until near the end of the semester, but I finally opened up and shared something that I had been struggling with. I was ready for rejection, but found instead a whole group of people that I had come to know and respect who gave me some very important, positive feedback. I found that what I was afraid of wasn't there; it was a very moving and important experience for me. If I had shared this with only one person, I probably would have heard some of the same things. But hearing it from eight other people—who didn't need to say it—was very powerful.

I drove home thinking, "I wonder what would happen if I

shared something like this with my wife?" The next day I told her about my experience in the group, and then I shared something about myself that I had never told anyone else. I was scared as I did, but Jan's response was incredible. Not only was she very understanding and affirming of me, she shared with me some things that she had never talked about with anyone as well. We had a great experience of intimacy and openness.

3. *You can "hitchhike" on someone else's work.*
About halfway through the semester in that group therapy class, the professor, during a quiet time in the group, asked me a question. She said, "Are you just out 'walking your dog,' or are you hitchhiking on what the others are doing?" I knew what she meant about "walking your dog," for she had asked someone else that before. She wanted to know if I was some-where else in my mind, or was I doing some internal work with myself as I listened to the other people. I assured her I was hitchhiking.

It's an interesting phenomenon in a group, to be there lis-tening to someone share and work through something that is very similar to one of your own issues. Sometimes you enter into the talking; other times you sit there silently examining your own experience to see how this relates to you. In other words, you don't have to be the center of the group's activity in order to benefit from what is going on. A good professional counselor leading the group will often notice when you are hitchhiking and ask you to share what's going on inside of you. This not only helps confirm things within you, it helps the others who are hitchhiking as well.

How to Find a Group

Finding a good support or therapy group isn't always easy to do. Whenever I suggest that someone attend a support group, I tell them to visit several and see which one seems like a fit. There are bad therapy groups, and there are bad support groups—at least for you. Someone else may find those groups helpful, but if they don't "fit" for you, they won't be helpful.

If you are looking for a good AA group, Al-Anon group, a sex-addiction group, Overcomers Outreach group, or some other organized support group, get a list of their meetings and attend several. See if people share things that indicate they are growing and finding help in the group. Look around and see if these are people you will enjoy being with on a weekly basis. If not, check out another group.

You can also call churches and ask what kind of support groups they offer in their weekly program. Some churches have different names for their support groups that have meaning for the members, but may not tell an outsider much about what the group is like. If that happens, ask the secretary what kind of group it is.

If you can't find a good group, consider starting one, especially if you have several friends struggling with the same kinds of problems. I wrote a book on perfectionism, and a number of people who read the book told me they started a group with other perfectionists to work on this issue. If you and several friends are struggling with a problem and there is a good book available on the subject, you can begin by slowly working your way together through the book.

In order to find a therapy group, you will have to talk with a professional counselor. If you're not working with a professional counselor, call several who have been recommended to you and ask if they have a therapy group, or if they know a good counselor who leads one. Usually the counselor will want to meet with you one-on-one before starting you in the group to see that your expectations coincide with those of the group.

Not every professional counselor leads a therapy group. I have led them when I worked in a hospital program, but I don't have any groups in my private practice. I enjoy leading groups, but usually don't have enough people at the same time who want to be in a group. I know several counselors who lead therapy groups and I usually suggest that people contact one of them to see if there would be a place for them.

Summary
- There is real value in meeting with a group of people; a powerful healing process can take place.
- There are two types of groups that work at different levels of intensity.
- Both types of groups aim to develop skills that will help people build healthier relationships.
- Be selective in choosing a group; not every group will be a good fit for every person.

Other Paths for Finding Help

TEN

Helping Ourselves by Helping Others

The last step of a twelve-step program says this: "Having had a spiritual awakening as the result of these steps, we tried to carry this message to others and to practice these principles in all our affairs." What this means is that a large part of a person's continued healing comes through helping others in the same process. It is much the same thing that Paul says in his Second Letter to the Corinthians:

All praise to the God and Father of our Lord Jesus Christ. He is the source of every mercy and the God who comforts us. He comforts us in all our troubles so that we can comfort others. When others are troubled, we will be able to give them the same comfort God has given us.

2 CORINTHIANS 1:3-4

A word of caution as we begin this section: We do not begin our search for help by helping others. This will not work. There are far too many people who try to help others thinking that they will somehow heal themselves in the process. It never seems to work. We cannot begin to help others until we have received help ourselves. Note what Paul says in the above passage: We are to comfort others with the comfort we have received. He does not say we are to comfort others so that we can be comforted. This is a big difference. We can only give what we have received, so we must wait and receive first.

Paul is also saying that we are helped *so that* we can in turn help others. Receiving help is not an end in itself. In fact, at that point our healing is incomplete. In Alcoholics Anonymous, the old-timers who call themselves twelfth-steppers say, "Our helping others is the best way we can *continue* to help ourselves." There are several people I call on when I come across someone who needs help with drinking or drug abuse. If I sound hesitant in asking them for help, they quickly remind me that helping these new people is often more help to them than to the other person. It's part of their own healing.

A friend of mine is always suggesting that we are to "turn our misery into a ministry." And many people have. I know of a young man who was caught up in an addiction to all kinds of perverse sexuality. He started early in high school and continued on into adulthood. His behavior covered just about everything possible and he was a miserable, lonely young man. Then God got hold of his heart and transformed him. As he went through a recovery from his sexual addictions, there came a point when God seemed to prompt him to begin a ministry to sex addicts. He started slowly since he didn't want to jeopardize his own recovery and healing. Over the years, he has built a large and effective ministry through publications, an Internet site, public speaking, and workshops. He has helped countless people break free from that addiction as he turned his misery into a ministry.

How Our Helping Others Helps Us

Obviously, helping others isn't where we begin our own healing process. Remember, it's the last step in the twelve-step
program of recovery. We must have experienced some degree
of healing within ourselves first, but we don't want to wait until
we are completely healed of our pain. Our full healing may
not take place until we reach out to help others. Then we find
full and complete release from our past. But how does helping others help us? Let's look at three ways that helping others continues the healing process that we have already begun.

1. *Helping others keeps us from getting lost in our pain.*
If we look only at our own problems and pain, we become preoccupied with ourselves. I've worked with several women who
have had multiple abortions that they deeply regretted later in
life. In many cases, their grief was intense and seemed to both
them and me to be endless. It was as if they were lost in their
pain and couldn't find a way out. For some, they had grieved
for years over the foolishness of their youthful decisions.
Several of them built their life around their past sin, and lived
so much in the past that they had nothing going on in the
present.

I suggested to one woman, who had grieved for years over
what she had done, that she might volunteer at a crisis pregnancy center and counsel some of the young women on the
threshold of making the same decision she had made years
before. She said she'd think about it, but she didn't do it right
away. After awhile, she stopped coming to counseling, mostly
out of frustration over her inability to break free from her past.
But I saw her a couple of years later and she was a different

woman. She almost glowed as she shared stories of the young women she had helped at the crisis pregnancy center. I had suggested this ministry but I had no way of knowing that she had actually started volunteering there. It was obvious that by helping others she had found the help she needed to complete her own grieving.

I talked with another woman who had become part of her church's ministry to women who had had abortions. She led a weekly support group and helped put together the annual retreats, even sharing her own story at some of the retreats. She had discovered that as she reached out to help others, she was able to finish her own grieving. Both of these women spent time in counseling, working on the issue of their own abortions, before they volunteered to work with other women. But in both cases, as in others as well, their reaching out to help others allowed them to complete their own healing and become more alive in the present.

2. *Helping others keeps us from getting lost in the past.*
Some people build their life around their past. They feel they need to remember everything in order to experience healing. I often warn these people about the dangers of becoming emotional archaeologists. It is dangerous to get so involved in our past emotional trauma that we feel like we need to research every event, and every nuance of every event, in order to break free. Instead, this focus leads to further bondage to the pain and problems of the past.

Emotional archaeologists have no life, for their present consists of analyzing and researching the past. Once people enter this mindset, they are unable to help others with their struggles. If someone comes to talk about a problem, emotional archaeologists quickly compare what the person is talking about with their own struggle. They manipulate the conversation so that the person who has come for help winds up trying to help instead.

Life is meant to be lived in the present. We need to understand our past so that we don't repeat negative patterns, but we want to be free to live in today. Finding the right balance between our past and our present is essential if we are to live life as God wants. King David gives us an example of this balance. When Nathan confronted him with his sin of adultery, David repented, but also faced some serious consequences. One of these was the death of the baby conceived in that illicit union.

When the baby became deathly sick, "David begged God to spare the child. He went without food and lay all night on the bare ground" (2 Samuel 12:6). David was not only grieving the child, he was grieving his own past and his sin. But when the baby died seven days later, David stopped grieving. His advisors were amazed. When they commented on this, David told them, "I fasted and wept while the child was alive, for I said, 'Perhaps the Lord will be gracious to me and let the child live.' But why should I fast when he is dead? Can I bring him back again? I will go to him one day, but he cannot return to me" (2 Samuel 12:22-23). David then went and comforted Bathsheba. Life went forward.

Now that may seem like a sudden change, and it certainly did to David's advisors. Most of us need more time than that. But David's behavior illustrates the principle that we need to deal with the past, and we also need to be alive in the present.

We need to spend time understanding the past, but we don't want to become a slave to it. Helping others keeps us from getting lost in our past.

3. *Helping others keeps our "story" from getting lost.*

When we have faced our own problems, and worked through the pain with the help of others, we have a valuable story to tell. We may feel shy or awkward about what we have to say. We may think that it is too trivial and couldn't possibly help someone else. We may even feel shame over what happened. But the story of our healing process can help others who are struggling with similar issues.

Both the woman who started volunteering at the crisis pregnancy center and the one leading the church's support group and retreats, felt ashamed of their story, and kept it secret for years. But their healing wasn't complete until they were able to open up and tell it to someone else.

Paul encourages us to reach out to others not only in his "comforting" passage, but in other places as well. In Galatians 6:1, he says, "If another Christian is overcome by some sin, you who are godly should gently and humbly help that person back onto the right path." You may say you are not godly enough, but if you are in the process of experiencing God's healing in your life, you fit the qualifications. Paul continues with the warning, "And be careful not to fall into the same temptation yourself. Share each other's troubles and problems, and in this way obey the law of Christ" (verses 1-2). We need to be careful, but we need to be available.

Sharing our story with someone who needs help also requires sensitivity on our part, not only to the other person, but also to the promptings of the Holy Spirit. We may want to forget parts of our story because they are too painful, but the pain can also be a reminder of God's grace and healing in our lives.

Paul reminds Titus, "Once we, too, were foolish and disobedient. We were misled by others and became slaves to many wicked desires and evil pleasures.... But then God our Savior showed us his kindness and love. He saved us, not because of the good things we did, but because of his mercy. He washed away our sins and gave us new life through the Holy Spirit" (Titus 3:3-5). Here Paul is sharing his own story with Titus, reminding him of his and Titus' growth beyond their past.

In the same way, our ability to humbly help others, and at the same time continue to help ourselves, stems from remembering where we have come from. God's love and mercy brought healing to us so we can be where we are today. That story can bring hope and healing to someone else.

Summary

Once we have moved forward in our own healing and in resolving our situation, we are uniquely equipped to help others in similar situations. Sarah was so encouraged by her divorce recovery workshop that she volunteered to take the training and become a facilitator for the next workshop. She wanted to give back because she felt she had received so much. She knew also that as she helped others face the pain in their lives, she would be helped as well.

It is important that we give back part of what we have received. In this way, we solidify the gains we have made in our own healing. It is also a responsibility we have. Paul doesn't make it an option when he tells us to comfort one another. It is simply presented as something we are to do.

But it is important that we don't reach out too quickly. We need to be most of the way through our own pain; our problem situation needs to be on its way to resolution. If we reach out too soon, we run the danger of hurting someone else because we are still hurting too much. The divorce recovery workshop leader suggested that Sarah sit through another workshop before taking a leadership role, just to be certain she was in a good enough place to be helpful to others. As she thought about it, she knew the leader was right. She didn't want to wait, but she didn't want to start too soon either.

ELEVEN

Healing Prayer

I know, you're thinking: Why isn't this chapter at the beginning? Isn't prayer the foundation for everything? And the answer is a resounding "YES!" Every form of help we have discussed to this point needs to be rooted and grounded in prayer. You, the one seeking help, need to be praying. And anyone you are turning to for help needs to be praying as well. We want to look at something a little different from that.

In this chapter, we want to look at some of the special ways prayer has helped people with problems, sometimes very serious problems. To better understand these paths of finding wise counsel, let's follow Scott again. Scott has been working hard in his therapy group for several months, but recently, he hasn't wanted to go. Marianne thinks he is sliding into his old behavior patterns. When she talks with Scott about this, he doesn't disagree, but also doesn't know what to do differently.

When Scott talked with his professional counselor, he didn't seem to think the situation was serious. He suggested they keep track of things and see what happened. That wasn't good enough for Marianne, who went and talked with a friend's pastor from a different church. He listened to her review what had been happening and suggested that Scott come in to see him. He added that they had a ministry team in their church who, when it seemed appropriate, would spend a day praying with someone. They called it "soaking prayer," and they had seen God bring some incredible victories in the lives of those who had participated. He would talk with Scott to see if he was an appropriate candidate for a day of soaking prayer.

What the pastor was suggesting for Scott was only one form of healing prayer. Over the years, there have been other ways people have experienced an intense time of prayer for a specific problem. Let's look at three of the most common ways.

1. Inner Healing Prayer

There are several ways to experience this type of prayer. For example, when our children were young, Jan and I simply prayed over them while they slept. We prayed very specifically for various aspects of their relationships and behaviors. But we also prayed that God would fill in the gaps where we had failed them in some way, even in ways we were unaware of. Our prayer, as we stood or knelt beside them, was more meaningful to us than prayer offered in their absence. We didn't neglect to pray for them at other times, we just wanted to add this type of prayer to what we were already doing.

Another form of prayer uses our sanctified imagination. I have led people in this prayer according to the following pattern. First, I ask them to get comfortable, to breathe deeply, and to relax. After a few minutes of this, I ask them to picture in their imagination their presence in some biblical scene. I often use the story of the four men who brought the paralytic man to Jesus and lowered him through the roof. I urge them to picture themselves as one of the four people carrying the man to the house where Jesus is teaching.

I then suggest that Jesus looks directly at them and calls

them by name as he leaves the house after the crowd disperses. After a brief greeting, the person is to remain in this imaginary scene and talk with Jesus in their thoughts, telling him about the specific problem they are facing. If they are dealing with a painful memory or situation, they are to ask Jesus to touch that hurtful place within them and to begin the healing process. Then I suggest they stay silent and listen to what Jesus says to them. After their conversation with Jesus ends, they are to finish as they would a prayer and thank him for meeting with them.

Afterwards, we talk together about what they experienced. It is usually a very moving time emotionally, for it is a powerful way to pray. I remind them that meeting Jesus like that is very real, for Jesus is not bound by time and space, and can actually meet us that way.

If you want to pray like this, you might want someone to guide you in the process. Otherwise, take some time to relax, then read a passage in the Gospels where Jesus is actively meeting with people. As you imagine yourself in that scene, the other people fade away and you are left alone with Jesus to talk with and listen to him.

2. Prayer for Healing

I once worked with a man who was deeply wounded emotionally by a bizarre childhood. His mother had done very strange things with him when he was in elementary school, and his father didn't seem to care. He just ignored the whole thing. From what my client remembered, it was easy to see why he struggled in his everyday adult relationships. I worked with him weekly for several years in one-on-one counseling sessions.

During this time, he also attended a church that was very open to people with a wounded past. Quite often, after the sermon, the pastor would ask any who wanted prayer to come to the front by the pulpit. There was a prayer ministry team that had been trained in this church, and they were there to individually pray with those who came forward.

These people on the prayer ministry team did more than pray for the person. They spent time talking with them first so that they would know specifically how to pray. Often, prayer team members prayed alone for a person, but sometimes they would invite another person from the team to join them. Obviously, they were not in a hurry to finish so they could get to lunch. Many times they were there with an individual for almost an hour, and two or three people from the team would gather around the person to pray.

Anne had this kind of experience. After she had dealt with her issues at work, she still had frustrating faith questions that she simply couldn't satisfy. She read helpful books and received advice that made sense at the time, but later the questions and doubts came back. Finally she asked for prayer, and several people from a similar prayer team at her church came to her house, laid hands on her, and prayed for her. She said it felt like an oppressive spirit had been lifted from her. The questions were gone.

She also received prayer every Sunday morning at her church. I watched her change dramatically over the almost three years we worked together. As we wound down her counseling, one of the things we discussed was how our counseling and the prayer she received almost every week had combined to bring about change and growth within her. I felt honored to be a part of what God had done in her healing, and knew that much of it came from the action of God through prayer.

3. Soaking Prayer

Scott experienced the third type of healing prayer. After he talked with the pastor, one of the prayer team leaders called and arranged to meet on a Saturday. They told him to plan on being there the whole day, and to arrange a ride so he wouldn't have to drive home. Then they suggested he make some notes about everything he could remember from his childhood.

He arrived for his Saturday appointment both excited and scared. He wasn't sure about what was going to happen, but he felt good about the pastor's explanation of the process. He came into the room, met the four members of the prayer team, and then sat down. One person sat with him, and the other three were seated separately from him. They opened the session in prayer together, and then the leader asked him about what he had written down.

Scott hardly noticed the other three people, but during that whole time they were praying. As the day progressed, they worked methodically through the events on Scott's list. At times, one of the team members stopped and asked a penetrating question that opened Scott's memory.

At different points during the day, the four gathered around Scott and prayed for him regarding specific periods of time in his life. After several hours, Scott's emotional wall broke down and he began to sob. Again, everyone gathered around, prayed, discussed what he was feeling, and then prayed some more. They prayed about bondage and about strongholds—the influence of the past and the grip of evil spirits. Scott wasn't sure he understood but the team, sensing his uncertainty, stopped and explained. As the day ended, they prayed for his release and healing, anointing him with oil as they prayed.

Scott had wondered why they had suggested someone bring him and pick him up, but now he knew: he was too exhausted to drive home. For several days he kept the experience to himself, not wanting to spoil it by talking about it. Then, as he realized how different he felt, he shared everything he could remember with Marianne. When he returned to his therapy group, others could see a marked change in him; after a couple of months, he no longer felt the need to attend the group.

Now, three years later, Marianne reports that they still have their problems, but she feels like she is married to a different person. He has held his job for three years, helps around the house, and acts "like a normal husband, finally." God cleared out some deep wounds within Scott through soaking prayer.

A counselor I know had a similar experience with a young woman she was counseling. The woman had had a horrible childhood, and she coped with it by creating separate parts of herself. She had what is typically called multiple personality disorder. She was so split emotionally that some of her personalities didn't know that she had other pesonalities. The counselor worked with her for some time and progress was very slow. Then the young woman heard of a church with a ministry team that did soaking prayer especially for women struggling with multiple personalities.

The young woman went to her day of soaking prayer, which was much like what Scott experienced. Among other things, the team prayed for the healing of the split part of her personality so that she would be integrated as one person. When the day was over, she was a changed woman. She told the counselor about what had happened, and of course, the counselor was skeptical. But over the next two months of counseling, this woman was different. She was whole. Soon, the counseling became unnecessary and ended.

The counselor was curious, of course, about the prayer ministry of this church. She was working with other women who had similar struggles. She met with the pastor and he told her many stories of people healed through the ministry of their soaking prayer team.

Summary

Not every person is comfortable with each type of healing prayer ministry, nor is every church equipped with people gifted by the Holy Spirit to lead this kind of ministry. And not every problem or situation will be resolved as successfully as Scott's, or the young woman's. But we should never limit God's ability to bring healing to our wounded parts through prayer.

Sometimes, though, God wants our healing process to take awhile, for there are truths he wants us to learn in the process. The story of King Saul offers an interesting example of this. When Saul is to be anointed king, he is too shy and too embarrassed to be seen. When Samuel announces that Saul is to be king, everyone looks around and they can't find him. Finally, they find him "hiding among the baggage" (1 Samuel 10:22).

Saul was obviously a fearful young man, but God knew what he could become. After he was made king, however, Saul simply returned home and resumed farming. Perhaps he wondered why he had made such a big deal about being king, why he was so fearful. But then, a month later, enemies besieged one of the cities of Israel and the people were help-less. They sent letters throughout the country asking for aid. When Saul heard what was happening, "the Spirit of God came mightily upon Saul, and he became very angry" (1 Samuel 11:6).

The fruit of the Spirit in this situation was anger. Anger is the opposite of fear. You cannot be angry and afraid at the same time. What God did here was give Saul a spiritual gift that offset some wounded part of himself. For the next four chapters, Saul is a mighty king. He is everything God knew he could become.

But then God gives Saul a very specific task to perform. Saul does part of the job and then lies about what he didn't do. Samuel is angry at Saul's disobedience and tells Saul "Obedience is far better than sacrifice" (1 Samuel 15:22). Saul pleads with Samuel, and admits why he disobeyed God: "I have disobeyed your instructions and the Lord's command, for I was afraid of the people and did what they demanded" (1 Samuel 15:24). When God filled Saul through the Holy Spirit with the ability to be angry, that spiritual gift offset his fearfulness. But Saul didn't learn what he needed to learn in order to hold on to that. God's gift was rendered null and void as Saul responded once again in fear. His character wasn't changed.

Saul's tragic story illustrates why God's healing of our woundedness often takes longer than we like. Apparently, there are things we need to learn at a deep interior level, in the depths of our character, as our healing proceeds. We would miss out on this vital transformation if our healing were instantaneous. That was Saul's experience, and it could be ours. Whether God heals us quickly, or allows us to work through our pain over time, there is something in his wisdom that is hidden from us and is related to his time frame.

We need to be patient in the process. We also must remember that God cares for us in the midst of our struggle, and that we usually meet him most profoundly when we meet him in our pain. Regardless of which path we take to find wise counsel, we should walk confidently because God walks with us down that path.

Notes

FIVE
Talking to Your Pastor or a Peer Counselor

1. Discussed in E.L. Worthington, Jr., *How to Help the Hurting* (Downers Grove, Ill.: InterVarsity, 1985), 15.
2. An excellent training program is the videotape series put out by the American Association of Christian Counselors, entitled "Helping People God's Way." Information can be obtained by visiting their web site, www.aacc.org, or by calling them at 1-800-526-8673.
3. Gary Collins, *Christian Coaching* (Colorado Springs: NavPress, 2002), 16.

SEVEN
How to Work With a Counselor

1. This discussion of the issue of trust is based in part on Erik H. Erikson, *Childhood and Society*, 2d ed. (New York: Norton, 1963).

EIGHT
Medications—Yes or No?

1. Much of this information is based on the columns written by Michael Lyles, M.D. in the periodical *Christian Counseling Today*. This quote is from Vol. 9, No. 2, 68.
2. Lyles, 69.
3. Based on Michael Lyles, "Shrink Notes," *Christian Counseling Today*, Vol. 9, No. 4, 66-67.